Arthritis – The Best Thing That Ever Happened To Me
(Healing The Pain Of Psoriatic And Rheumatoid Arthritis And How Autoimmunity Can Heal Your Body And Soul)

PHIL ESCOTT

Copyright © 2012 PHIL ESCOTT
All rights reserved.
ISBN:9781976938948

Contents

Foreword by Gabrielle Heyes..i
Foreword by Dr. Jack Kruse...iii
Introduction...viii

Part One – The Beast
CHAPTER 1 – It All Goes Horribly Wrong..1
CHAPTER 2 – The Lyme Disease Fiasco..15
CHAPTER 3 – A Ray of Hope..21
CHAPTER 4 – Rediscovering My Father..29
CHAPTER 5 – Getting Serious...35
CHAPTER 6 – Beyond Diet And Into The Cold..............................51

Part Two – Taming the Beast
CHAPTER 7 – So What Do I Do Exactly?...65
CHAPTER 8 – Diet In Detail...79
CHAPTER 9 – Other Areas To Look At..99

Part Three – The Nature of the Beast
CHAPTER 10 – First Awakening...125
CHAPTER 11 – Second Awakening..139
CHAPTER 12 – Third Awakening...155
CHAPTER 13 – The Blessing of Suffering..165
CHAPTER 14 – My Healing Journey in Words and Pictures.......171

Conclusion and Testimonials..175

FOREWORD BY GABI HEYES, NATUROPATH, HERBALIST AND IRIDOLOGIST

I read Phil's book with great amusement as I recalled some of the wacky things he did in his quest to heal himself. The overriding sense in his journey is his determination (or stubbornness)! Not one to give up, he used his wit, hunger for knowledge and cynicism to find the answers that made sense physically for the body. He has a deep understanding of the complexities of human emotion and how positive thoughts create higher vibratory frequencies that permeate the lower to create wellness.

When Phil came to see me at my clinic he was an overweight hippy (ok, he's still a hippy) with really cool dreadlocks that were long enough to skip with. The second visit I walked right past him as he sat there with his son – a shaved head and half the man. The third visit he was a positively buff-looking 50-year-old!

Phil has always strived for enlightenment in its true sense, but I believe that enlightenment can occur on any level, and for him it was a combination of discoveries that led him away from the medical field and into his own – listening to his needs.

He understands the naturopathic principle that the body will heal itself given the right means – a true believer – but most of all an experimenter. This book made me laugh, and I love the way Phil tried some bizarre things, yet didn't quit, and in this process has helped other people to 'wake up' to their own bodies – to the great achievements that are possible with the right guidance.

I believe this book will resonate with so many who have had the same disheartening, negative experiences and advice with their condition. It offers a message of hope, belief and self-empowerment. Enjoy your journey!

FOREWORD BY DR. JACK KRUSE, NEUROSURGEON AND VISIONARY

Humans enter this world and awaken to a simple truth: First we must find our voice to flourish. Second, we must find our story within this great epic of being that we call life, and we must do this before we exit life. Phil seems to have gotten that message from the universe.

Like us all, Phil ascribed to the precepts of what could bring him health, and he found that most of what he was told enriched others but just left him more broken. The medicine man's chronic wallet biopsies did not bring him solace, but discomfort. Instead of viewing that stress as a misfortune, he used that discomfort to innovate a change in himself by changing his priorities. Any misfortune 'that lies outside the sphere of choice' should be considered an opportunity to strengthen our resolve, not an excuse to weaken it. How did he become stronger when he was weaker? He did what steel does to become stronger. He added ideas to his own recipe of madness to create brilliance.

Why should you risk sharing your precious ideas? When you engage your own mind, imagination takes you to places where the prescription of optimal lies for you. You must trust your instincts. Why must you? Because you can trust that a better idea might surface after that initial plunge. An idea, like any wave, when thrown into a bigger body of water creates a powerful wave of momentum that might change the world.

Our success rises and falls on human connections, not on wisdom alone. Phil came on my forum and shared his story long before this book was written. At that moment he had me at hello. Convergence can lead to innovation by a chance moment in time. I found my own wellness Rx in the most unlikely of places; it was in the world of quantum physics. And that story is how Phil and I became entangled.

To flourish, you must taste failure. Phil's story reveals that tale. We learn best from our own failures if we are wise. We all have our own vision of what we should be. Usually, that sight is burned in our retinas FOREVER. Most have always wanted to live far from the madding crowd and be self-sustaining. That vision in your mind requires action. Most become are devoid of passion because their version of ideation is done without execution; and that has led to deletion of most of our greatest ideas and visions. This is where we begin to rely on so-called "experts". I used to be one of those so-called "experts" as a neurosurgeon, until I evolved my ideas via actions.

Evidence based medicine is based upon "hard scientific evidence." How many of us have heard that very same phrase throughout our careers in medicine? Most of us have used it many times. And when we did, we really had no idea what it implies. In the beginning of my career I had just naturally regarded "hard scientific evidence" as if it were more or less a tangible object we could handle physically or mentally; tangible like the Statue of Liberty, Big Ben and the Mona Lisa. It had never occurred to me that recognizing "hard scientific evidence" would be any more difficult than recognizing the statue, the clock, or the painting. Only much later did I realize that "hard scientific evidence" was only an amorphous concept, not a concrete precept.

I like connecting with people who think or at least have open minds. I have no time for those who cannot entertain the nonconformist view. Conventional wisdom serves to protect others from the painful job of thinking. Being open-minded shows the willingness to consider the evidence presented, but not the willingness to accept the claims without any evidence. Evidence however, requires asking the correct questions to expose the blind spot of the question. In that shadow is usually where nature's rules exist. That is the sliver of light where I found wisdom. I left my knowledge and education behind in the darkness of the expert I used to be. You cannot rely on anyone to change your personal thunderstorm. This is the source of our discontent. When we become usurped, we have not prioritized things in our life. The beliefs of modern man are the batteries that make them fuel for the matrix in which they live.

Time is the only wealth we're given.

No one can stop a ticking clock... but the best of us figure out how to slow it down. Anytime you slow light you become capable of slowing time.

Phil learned that lesson well, as you will soon see.

New ideas like these can be quite fragile at their outset. When we first unleash them on the world they can be minimized by a "yawn"; they can also be slowly bled to death by a sharp comment, or killed by a facial frown. But when an idea is really special, it is a rude awakening to the new dawn's sleepy eyes. A new idea is like a beautiful sunrise; it begins whispering to the world that something new is happening on the world's stage for the very first time. It's time for you to wipe the sandman from your eyes and wake up to this reality. Put some action behind your vision and watch your power animate your vision.

Spare your advice for those who value it by using it. Phil did, and I adore him for that. I hope his words contained within his work here will inspire you to create your inner masterpiece. Many of you may not believe you have greatness buried in your scrap heap.

Do you think we just awaken from sleep? Could a change in priority, action, or thought change our DNA? Today, modern life has managed to numb our senses while we are conscious. Maybe your early family was helpful in training you to be submissive to control the animal within? The more you contain "an animal" the more ferocity they use to escape. The more risks they take. Ask Phil; he unleashed his dragon.

Too often in journeys to build a masterpiece the risks are often taken at the wrong time for the wrong reasons. Don't let risks taken at the wrong time harness your adventurous exploration. Where's your sense of adventure right now, people? Phil is getting ready to share some intimate details of risk-taking and trial and error with the world in a book.

There is a lesson in risk-taking for the wise. Works like this are for the wise among us. They begin to pay attention to something that can fundamentally shift a life. When you listen within what happens to the facade?

Now you sense your world is beginning to open inside out and bottom up, and the fog on your eye lifts so you can see the new world order unfolding in front of you. We already contain everything we need, people. Ask Phil. You need no drugs, no supplements, no cryotherapy and no expert opinion. There is no need for self-improvement. These are "the trips" we lay on our psyche; they are like clouds that temporarily block the sun. But all the time, our warmth and brilliance remain around us hidden from perception. This is who we really are. We are one blink of an eye away from being fully awake.

Many great ideas have been lost because the people who had them could not stand being laughed at when they begin. Me, I have no issues because I laugh at myself all the time. I love being called mad. Madness is where I connected to physics and nature.

The paradigm wants no action and creates priority confusion. You are devoid of the "passion to change" your patterns because your current precept of truth is prioritized by society. Think for yourself and use your brain's ability to see patterns and trends to act. Ideation is without execution... and that has led to deletion of our ideas and vision. This is the source of our discontent in medicine. We have not prioritized things in our life for years now.

TB is still a disease than can be cured by light. Why don't we use it? Because you cannot patent full spectrum sunlight that contains purple and red light. Wellness is built around three things: light, water, and magnetism. It is our job to figure out how to do so. The key always comes back to light. Light rides a surf board called EZ water and the waves we surf are created by electric and magnetic field in the environment around us. We create the waves in our environment 24/7 now, and we never even think that maybe we might be our own worst enemy? What is the take home message from Phil? Humans are not broken, but the environment they have built is ruining them.

    What is my take home message? Sunrises and sunsets are clinics dispensing free care. Physics drives our biology and opens the door to the compound pharmacy in our pituitary. Every sunset is a reset; every sunrise collapses a new waveform. When you live in an optimized environment with ideal optics, most ailments can be cured; time can be slowed using light while surgery can repair the environment. Putting Windex on your glass eye is brain surgery without a scalpel. Everyone looks to the future... their future. This is very shortsighted because we've gone too far from where we came from, and that's what we are looking for.

    Master the ego, embrace your fears, your anxieties, your darkest thoughts and channel them into the requisite energy and emotional intensity of nature.

    The only person who can help you is you. Ready yet?

INTRODUCTION

I never wanted to be a health expert; it was thrust upon me. I always had an interest in health, but, not having had to put any of the more accepted theories on diet and lifestyle to the test, I trotted out the same as everyone else believes – the "party line" – and when it came to the crunch, those theories were clearly flawed.

To heal myself I had to search for knowledge that is normally buried under the tide of nonsense that passes for sensible, balanced advice, but the body, when badly out of balance, needs something extreme to set it on the healing path again. Well, to many it might seem extreme, but when you get the hang of it, it's just a way to return the body to a stress-free state so it can correct these imbalances, as it is designed to do, chemical-free.

This book is the story of how I went from being a frightened bundle of pain and inflammation, confined to the couch, to the surprising place I find myself today, a place of ease and comfort I never thought I would see.

Since then I have had the utter privilege of working with many people both in person and all over the world via Skype and email, and I have seen them also find health again. I have seen inflammatory arthritis reversed in six weeks when one brave and trusting person put everything into it from the first day and covered all bases at once. I cannot guarantee it will be as quick for you – it certainly took me a lot longer. We all heal at our own rate and learn the lessons unique to us, but I can promise you great improvements whatever pace you go at.

Every day I thank the universe for giving me the gift of seeing so many smiling faces as they realise that the traditional gloomy diagnoses are nonsense and that their illness is not only curable, but might well be the making of them.

A word of warning: I will cover certain areas, particularly in the third part of the book, which might seem a little esoteric and not applicable to your situation if you are newly diagnosed and/or are not of a so-called spiritual nature. However, bear with me, and if it doesn't resonate right now, follow the advice in the first two parts, which should open you up to some minor miracles and give you confidence, and then at that stage, come back and delve into the subtler areas to find the real magic...

So, to business... You've been diagnosed with an autoimmune condition, and it's all pretty scary. Let's be brutally honest – you have two options...

1. You panic, wanting to be cured immediately with a magic bullet and go down the allopathic route of giving away your power to the doctor and taking the drugs. If you're lucky they might block the symptoms for a while, but you will be living in fear that they will return or worsen, now with the added fear that the drugs will damage other systems in your body, which, sooner or later, they surely will. This is not healing.

2. You can accept that you have this condition, accept that you probably caused it yourself with years of stress/neglect/misuse, and that it will take your body quite some time to heal. This can be very difficult to accept, but it's actually the start of a magical journey that will lead you not only into physical healing, but into areas of yourself that you might not even know existed. In the end you will arrive at such wholeness, with no fear of your past illness returning or any future illnesses developing and a total integration of your physical, emotional and spiritual sides. This is true healing.

Do I have all the answers to your problems? No, I don't, but the great news is that YOU do! However, in this book I will give you many ideas from my own experiences of the journey from initial panic to eventual healing and suggestions for further research that will hopefully help you to my one goal here – to inspire you to develop your own intuition and your understanding of your own body and the signs it gives you about what it needs to aid its own healing process.

So, do you have to suffer with the symptoms you already have? Maybe they seem unbearable right now, and the temptation to take the drugs is almost impossible to resist. Well, I can show you natural methods that will bring down the symptoms to a minimum so you can at least relax enough to work on the deep-seated causes, but still be able to read them. Symptoms are a necessary part of healing; they are your body's warning lights, so don't let your doctor cover them all up with drugs. If you took your car to the garage with the oil light on and the mechanic just smashed the bulb with a hammer, would you pay him? I doubt it!

You will come to realise on this journey that symptoms are all we really need to read what the body needs. As we learn to listen more carefully and make little steps of progress, we will gain confidence and the progress will speed up.

Be warned though, that the path of self-healing takes courage, and it's never straight. Sometimes you will be discouraged by setbacks and think you are on the wrong track, but take heart – there are no straight lines in nature, and your path to healing will not be linear. When there are setbacks, just trust the body and let it do what it needs – it is far wiser than any doctor. If you support it in its healing, it will eventually reward you with a level of health you never thought possible. When the going gets tough, there are two keys to success on the journey you are embarking on, and which you should always remind yourself of: TRUST and SURRENDER.

I have always been disorganised and unfocused. All through my life I made a point of starting things but never finishing them. If I liken my whole persona to a car, I had all the pieces necessary to build the car, but I had no nuts and bolts to hold them together. I'd studied meditation, diet, exercise etc, but I was off track. It took me the best part of three years of hard work to decipher the root cause of what was wrong with me, and that's the story I'd like to share with you. If this account seems a bit self-indulgent it's because in my own healing journey I always found the personal accounts of the successes of others to be the most inspiring, and they always held my butterfly attention like clinical explanations never could.

I have had to write some parts of my life that I'd rather not have written about – parts that quite possibly don't paint me in a very good light, and some I am very well aware even make me look like an idiot. However, accepting and working on those damaging patterns and traits in ourselves can be a massive key to healing, which is why I have included them. Perhaps by the admission of many of my faults I can show you how to accept yourself, change the things you can, and end up loving the rest, warts and all. None of us are, or ever will be, perfect. Just enjoy who you are! We are all idiots in our own ways.

So, this is the story of the roundabout route I took to find those nuts and bolts one-by-one and finally put the "car" together again on all levels – physical, emotional and spiritual. This book is split into three parts to deal with what I see as the three stages of my healing: the initial horror and confusion, finding ways to ease the symptoms and then getting to the root cause, or, as I have called the three parts of the book – The Beast, Taming the Beast and The Nature of the Beast.

* * *

My story starts off in a bit of a depressing time for me, so I thought I'd begin with an overview of what good health actually is, to give you something positive to inspire you from the off before you get swept up in the initial horror of my story, which, if you have just been diagnosed with something autoimmune, might very well have a lot of similarities to yours.

So what is good health? There is a common view that good health is defined as the absence of disease, or even more pessimistically, as the covering up of disease symptoms with chemicals. This is selling ourselves so short of our true potential that we have forgotten what true health is.

Health is not fitness, that's for sure, even though health and fitness have become so inextricably linked in people's minds. Many athletes are so overtrained and burned out that however spectacular they may look on the outside, the inside is a complete mess.

Health is not happiness either. Happiness is a fleeting emotion brought about by all sorts of internal and external factors and will always come and go, usually at direct odds with one's efforts to maintain it.

So, what is health? Above all, health is the free flowing of energy on all levels of our being – physical, energetic, emotional and spiritual. It's the smooth functioning of the mitochondria in the cells, the free exchange of electrons, the balanced play of the emotions and the ability to dive deep into the absolute nature of reality. Like the proverbial blade of grass left standing after the storm that felled the mighty oak tree, health is about being flexible and adaptable; to have the wonderful ability to slap oneself on the forehead every day and say, "I was wrong..." Health is not a fixed point either, but the ability to flow with changes and cycles, just like the rest of nature and to be free to remove energetic blockages as one goes along.

Even the best ideas we have had, or the most beneficial habits we have developed, should be open to change and improvement as circumstances around us and within us change. In this way we can live in the present, in harmony with our environment, and only then will we feel true health. When we achieve this, we will function smoothly on all levels and come to a state of such deep contentment and peace that next to it happiness is a very insignificant bonus.

As Ram Tzu once put it so beautifully... "Bring me your most cherished beliefs, and if you are really fortunate, you might leave without them." I hope my story inspires and helps you, and that it helps you reach your goals much more quickly and smoothly than I did.

I wish you every success!

Phil Escott

PART ONE
The Beast

⊃ **Chapter 1**
IT ALL GOES HORRIBLY WRONG

It was surprisingly painless as the needle slid through the synovial membrane of my ballooned left knee, and the doctor drained not one, but two massive syringes of lime green fluid. Looking past the knee, both ankles were also swollen and misshapen. The pain of getting up from the examination table would be far worse than the procedure itself, and I wasn't looking forward to it. It was surreal. How had I ended up here? I was fit and strong; I was a calm, spiritual yogi type, weight trainer and mountain biker for god's sake. This kind of thing happened to other people. I became aware of the doctor addressing me…"Of course your joints will never be "normal" again and you will have to take medication for the rest of your life… but try not to worry too much." Oddly, I wasn't that worried. Not yet anyway. I'd get rid of this inconvenience pretty quickly…

I looked over at the beautiful faces of my partner, Detta, and two-year-old daughter, Amelia, harshly illuminated by the ever-present hospital fluorescent lighting under which it's a wonder anyone ever recovers from anything. Amelia was fascinated, as children always are, and peered around the doctor to get a better view, wrinkling her nose in fascinated horror as the syringe filled up. Detta, a nurse herself, seemed to be doing her best to look positive with a reassuring smile. Inside I was strangely numb. It was hard to take it all in, so to lighten things, I made some stupid joke about the fluid looking radioactive and using the steroids I was about to be prescribed to get down to the gym and end up looking like Arnold Schwarzenegger.

Despite my optimistic banter, and despite a life of health and fitness, it would be a long time before I picked up a barbell again.

In fact, it would be a long road to recovering not only the health I had always taken for granted, but in many ways, it was the beginning of another kind of recovery. In what would become a three-year odyssey of excruciating joint pain and the Sherlock Holmes-like sleuthing for a solution, I also discovered something I had no idea I was even looking for – my sudden onset autoimmune condition would become a portal into a new way of relating to my body, and with it, my soul.

* * *

I was 48 years old, and it was somewhere around October 2010 when my first ankle exploded. I remember hearing a click in the joint, which was probably irrelevant, while putting a shoe on, and a couple of hours later I was in agony with a balloon for a right foot. At first I thought it was an old injury flaring up again from when I had fallen awkwardly from an indoor climbing wall some years previously and damaged the tendons and ligaments in my ankle, but after a couple of days it was swollen to the point that my toes had gone numb, and I knew something was seriously amiss.

The clues were there: for a year or so previously I had been popping Ibuprofen like sweets to unsuccessfully combat severe pain in my back, swallowing a pack of antacids per day, and I'd had a bout of iritis in the spring, which should have immediately suggested an autoimmune problem, but it would be years before I really put together what is now to me a very simple puzzle. It's funny how we get used to certain niggling ailments and ignore the symptoms. Our bodies are so eloquent as they warn us of how badly we are treating them, but in the west we are just not taught to listen to its wisdom. We are under the thrall of the young science of allopathic medicine, which takes away our power and puts it all in the hands of our doctors. I certainly hadn't been listening to my body for decades...

I had built up an impressive portfolio of ailments over the years and just got used to them one by one. I was getting very overweight too, but had this odd sort of body dysmorphia that told me I was still the reasonably lean and well-muscled chap who owned and ran a gym back in the late 90s... but I wasn't. Some of the muscle was still there, but it was so swathed in blubber that when I look back at photos now, I am astonished that I never realised how far it had gone.

I had also been plagued with hot flushes and rosacea for a decade, which were the bane of my life and seriously limited my every activity. I am a drummer, and I had to have a fan blowing in my face constantly just to make playing gigs bearable. I'd even choose one supermarket over another because it was a couple of degrees cooler, and I might just manage to get round and do all the shopping without seriously overheating and getting to the checkout with a sweaty, crimson and burning face. It is clear to me now that my whole system was very inflamed, and it is no wonder that it eventually collapsed.

Looking back, it is unbelievable that I ignored the symptoms for so long. I might have understood if I had been an average guy who had no real interest in health, but I had always been interested in diet and fitness. It is also astonishing to me that the doctors missed what was going on. It's not as if I didn't go to them; I did, but in all the time that my blood markers came back with elevated CRP and SED rates, showing that the body was in a state of inflammation, they never mentioned any way in which I could treat it. I later came to realise it's because they just don't know.

If I could go back in time to about 1999 when the first of the inflammatory markers started to show through, I could probably nip it in the bud in about two months with what I know now... But clearly I had to be that stupid so I could write this book, which I sincerely hope will help many people facing the same issues, because if there's a wrong turn that can be taken or a physical symptom that can be ignored, I've been guilty of them all! Right, back to late 2010... I could barely walk on my right ankle, and it was so swollen that I couldn't even get a regular shoe on. I remember going to the local medical walk-in centre (or hobble-in for me that day) to see if they had any suggestions. The best insight I got that day was from the triage nurse who asked to take a look at my fingers and spotted what I later learned are called Heberden's nodes on the tip joints, which had appeared in my thirties, painlessly, so I never bothered with them. She said that it showed that I was prone to arthritis and that my ankle might just be inflammatory arthritis. I didn't really take it in, but it was my first hint of what was to come.

On the way out I bumped into my favourite GP, a Dr Tekle, who used to work in my local surgery. I told him that I might have arthritis and he just said, "It's from how we've lived..." They were the first and last wise words I got from anyone associated with the UK's National Health System (NHS)... Dr Tekle has been sorely missed since he left my local practice and now works as a locum I think, but he always used to bemoan the demise of traditional cures, and he was the only doctor I'd ever run into who had respect for the old healing modalities. He was a breath of fresh air. The simple wisdom in his statement that day didn't really hit home with me either, as I still didn't believe that I was in trouble. I was still caught up in the misapprehension that there would be a pill I could take that would make it all go away. After all, serious illness was for other people... wasn't it?

A week or so later, my other ankle suddenly went the same way, and one day soon after, while squatting down to attend to some part of my drum kit, I noticed that my left knee was feeling a little "odd". By the next morning I also had a knee like a balloon. What the hell was going on? Three joints trashed in two weeks?

Where was this going to end? I started sleeping on the couch, as climbing stairs was so painful, and I was so fatigued that I'd just pass out in the early evening while watching television anyway. My lovely partner Detta would tuck me in, and the next thing I'd know it was midnight and I'd need to pee, and so would begin the excruciatingly slow and painful journey to the toilet, after which I'd return to the sofa for a restless night of pain and worry.

There were other symptoms too. I had various skin eruptions and rashes including a patch of very painful psoriasis on the palm of my right hand that made it look like it was rotting. I had fevers and cold sweats at night, and the fatigue and brain fog were debilitating. I had all sorts of digestive issues, having been told that I had hiatus hernia, and I had also been put on some nasty stuff called Lansoprazole, a proton-pump inhibitor to stop the indigestion and acid reflux. I believe that the combination of that, Ibuprofen and antacids was the last straw for my gut flora and set off the whole cascade, but we'll come to that. I also had a fatty liver, cysts on the liver, cysts on the kidneys, calcifications of arteries and prostate... the list goes on and on.

I was fortunate in one respect though: I had a fairly easy lifestyle at the time, having saved up some money. This enabled me to lie on the couch for many hours a day researching on the Internet and reading up on anything I could get my hands on. Somebody who had to hold down a regular job might well have been forced to submit to the prescription drugs just to be able to support the family. I feel deeply for those people, and one of the main aims of writing this book is to help those who have far less time to research than I did.

The first book I bought and read was "Conquering Arthritis" by Barbara Allen. I remember getting my first realistic glimmer of hope that it was truly possible to cure the "incurable". Barbara sets out a very detailed guide to all the factors that she thinks contributed to her arthritis and the steps she took to heal. It is mostly concerned with physiological approaches, but it gave me a start. It was clear from the outset that wheat was a huge problem for many ailments, and Barbara cites her final piece of the puzzle as an ingredient in her toothpaste that she had missed that contained wheat.

It's funny though that even when we are in pain and solutions are staring us in the face, it can still take a lot of time before we actually listen and implement them. It was even more daft in my case, as I knew the problems associated with wheat and dairy, but I still dragged my heels all those years thinking a little was okay (and ended up eating a hell of a lot). For a while I experimented with supposedly healthier options like gluten free flour, spelt flour, Ezekiel bread, quinoa and other "safe grains", but it was clear that they still aggravated the problem.

I missed the point of Barbara's book to a great extent, and decided that I should veer towards very strict veganism. At least I gave up most grains, but I was still eating Basmati rice and doing a lot of juicing and smoothies with green leaves and fruit. I had been a vegetarian for many years back in the eighties and early nineties, but then when I had taken up training with weights my body had cried out for more protein. I had started to eat chicken again, and felt very guilty about it, as I had the brainwashing so common amongst people of a "spiritual" bent that meat of any kind is somehow harmful. I also had the notion that I needed to "detox" and purify the system, as there must be something nasty in my physiology that it was reacting to – some sort of horrendous buildup of sludgy toxins that needed to be expelled by massive amounts of liquid sugary fruit juices. This is not at all how I see it now, but at the time, the conditioning kicked in, and I had to go down that path.

The one thing that really did work was fasting, just as Barbara Allen had written about. Of course, knowing about Ayurveda and being interested in healing for a long time, I had tried fasting before and knew that it brought results. After just two days of fasting on water only, the inflammation was hugely improved, and I also started to get obsessed with raw food... and not just the stuff I was juicing. I didn't enjoy the diet much, but still had it stuck in my head that if vegetarian was good, then raw veganism must be the ultimate.

I have to admit I did see some improvement, probably down to ditching the wheat and dairy, and I could go for short, uncomfortable walks, but progress was slow. A side benefit was that the excess weight that I had been carrying for years started to melt away. Looking back, I lost a lot of muscle around that time, but still carried a lot of the fat, so things weren't as positive as they seemed at first on the bathroom scales.

I was also masking the symptoms, mostly unsuccessfully, with Ibuprofen and Paracetamol. I was also still having horrible brain fog and dizziness, which I could easily explain now, given what I was eating and the chemicals I was taking, but I didn't really put the evidence together at the time.

Finally I got my first appointment with a rheumatologist, and I shuffled along to see him, still thinking I'd be cured in a week or so. He turned out to be a very nice guy called, for the purposes of this book, "Dr. B". Dr. B examined me and told me a few pessimistic things that day, three of which stuck in my head, and it would be years before I managed to get rid of those little negative "affirmations". He said that my joints would never be "normal" again, that I would have to take medication for the rest of my life and that nothing worked except for their pills; no diet or natural cures would have any effect. I was in good spirits and laughing and joking during that appointment, even as he aspirated the previously mentioned greenish fluid from my knee. I think I was still in denial despite what he was telling me and still thought I'd find a way out very fast. Actually, in the months and years ahead I never lost that belief, but I just became more realistic about the timescale and complexity of such a cure. Dr. B's comments that day didn't help, even though I know he meant well.

He did however offer one tiny straw to clutch at, telling me it might be reactive arthritis and it might go in a few months. Reactive arthritis, for those who don't know, is a short-term bout of inflammation preceded by, commonly, chlamydia or some sort of stomach bug. I had suffered a long bout of diarrhoea a few weeks previously, so he said that it might be down to that, but only time would tell. To me, that is a clear indication that it has something to do with the gut, but allopathic medicine still does not seem to see this. In the meantime he suggested that I took steroids and a drug called Sulfasalazine for about six months, and then see if the inflammation had gone. If it had, it was reactive arthritis, but if it hadn't it was more serious. I wasn't keen on taking drugs and went away to think about it.

Already, after that first consultation, things were not adding up to me. When I went in I thought I was going to see somebody who knew how to cure the ailment that was their particular area of expertise, but it soon became clear that rheumatologists knew nothing about the cause of arthritis and offered no cures. This made no sense to me. I mean, if you called a plumber out to fix a leaky pipe and he said that he had no idea why the pipe was leaking and couldn't fix it, you would be very unlikely to pay him, but in the field of medicine this is going on all the time, and not only do doctors get well paid, but they get practically deified. I am thankful for my long-standing problem with any sort of authority, which at the time was all I really had to cling to. From that first day I knew I'd find a way out, but at the time I had no idea how.

I didn't believe Dr. B that it was incurable for two reasons: Firstly, it made no sense to me that the process of inflammation within the synovial membranes of joints was incurable and could not be reversed when reactive arthritis existed. Surely the only difference between reactive arthritis and rheumatoid or psoriatic arthritis, the types that are supposed to be incurable, was that the cause of the reaction was taken away in reactive arthritis – the chlamydia or stomach bug. It was just down to me to find out what the cause was in my own body. It seemed to me that any arthritis was reactive – one just had to pin down what the body was reacting to.

Secondly, my father had been diagnosed with rheumatoid arthritis in the 1950s. They gave him gold injections and told him he'd eventually be in a wheelchair, but by 1960 he had moved to Jordan and the joint pain had totally disappeared, never to return between then and 2003 when he died, aged 77. This was supposed to be impossible, but I knew it had happened, so it gave me confidence. For most of my life I thought that if it ever happened to me all I would need to do would be to move to a hot country and it would go away. Much later I realised that the climate probably had very little to do with why my father's problems disappeared. I will go into that later, but for the time being my father's cure showed me that it was possible to heal, and allowed me not to take it too seriously when the rheumatologists told me it wasn't.

I returned home after that first appointment with a lot to think about. I started to research into cures for arthritis and found a massive quagmire of conflicting information online. I can understand why at this point many would also give up and throw themselves 100% into the hands of their doctors, as it is all very confusing, and of course doctors are hardly ever supportive if you tell them you have been Googling symptoms and cures. Even though they can't cure these chronic ailments, they sincerely believe that they are the world authorities on the subject. This isn't the case, but one has to do a lot of digging to find those that do know how to help.

I remember Christmas 2010 being a time of deep depression and pain. I could not enjoy my lovely daughter Amelia, then only two years old, and what should have been the first Christmas she could actually appreciate was full of thoughts that I might not be around to see her grow up. So many bodily systems seemed to be affected that I could hardly believe that this mortal coil would put up with it for long and I would soon shuffle it off. People think of arthritis as a little bit of joint pain, but when it's autoimmune in origin the effects reach far beyond the joints and can be devastating. My relationships were suffering too, and not just with Amelia. Detta had the patience of a saint with me and was so loyal and supportive, but it was clear that the witty, carefree guy she had met was a thing of the past, and I was depressed, hostile and certainly no fun to be around. At the time we lived in a big house with my mother there too, as I had looked after her since my father died. She was not an easy person to get on with – very disapproving and set in her ways. I could barely take care of myself, let alone her, and the resentments that had already been building over previous years came to a head. Not only did I feel as ill as I did, but I felt like I was trapped and had wasted the last good years of my life looking after her, with little or no appreciation from her at all. I became very bitter, and it was not a happy household. It felt like my life was over, and to have to end my life in such pain was not conceivable for me. Although on one level it was indeed happening, I still clutched onto the idea that I would find a way out, however gloomy the outlook was on the face of it.

By January 2011, I was getting desperate. It seemed like an eternity that I had been ill, and if I had known at the time how long the road ahead of me would be, total despair would have overcome me, I'm sure. I decided to contact Dr. B again and have a go at his pharmaceuticals just until I had it under control naturally. I couldn't take the constant pain any more.

Dr. B put me on Prednisolone, the UK name for the steroid prednisone, and within a couple of days the inflammation was miraculously reduced to a small fraction of what it had been. I could walk with minimal discomfort, and it was heaven. Any pain was only there for a short time in the morning until the next pills kicked in, and for the first time in a couple of months life was bearable again. I fell into the trap of thinking that I was cured, and even though I had read a great deal about how steroids were only a short-term stopgap and very dangerous, I would be the one who would be cured by them. My nightmare was over! Wahey! Hmm...At the time I was in a band. The months from October to December were obviously difficult for the band, as I was in no state to do anything, and they didn't really understand what was happening to me. However, with the false hope of the steroids I remember clearly on the 19th January going out with the guys to see another band.

It was so good to be thinking of something other than how agonising my joints were, and the simple act of being able to walk up and down stairs was such a joy. I also remember clearly that it was the last time I ever smoked a cigarette. I was never a heavy smoker, but on social occasions I would sometimes have a few, and that evening I just wanted to forget that my body was in crisis and be able to abuse it like everyone else. It was a great evening, and I felt so happy for the first time in ages. I went to bed that night a very happy chappy.

Morning came, and I couldn't even get out of bed. I couldn't believe it. I took Ibuprofen and the steroids, but still by midday I was crippled. I looked back at the previous evening and blamed it on the smoking, but I had no idea really what had happened. I was utterly devastated. The new lease of life I had been given had now cruelly been snatched away from me, and I was in hell again, now even losing faith in the false security of the drugs.

I put up with it for a while, occasionally pestering the nurses at the rheumatology department on the phone who would talk to Dr. B and then call back telling me to up the Prednisolone dosage, pop more Ibuprofen, put ice on the joints and elevate them and other useless advice. Looking back I am utterly astonished that nobody ever mentioned diet except to say that it's always best to lose weight, as it would lessen the pressure on the joints (no mention of it reducing inflammation). Of course, the NHS still think that one should lose weight by calorie counting, eating whole grains and watching your fat intake, so it's no wonder that not only do their diets never work, but people never stick to them, so they don't even bother to mention it in the end.

Eventually, around the beginning of February, if I remember correctly, I went to see Dr. B again. He had been trying to get me to take a nasty substance called Sulfasalazine, a drug that supposedly shuts down the onslaught of the immune system in the joints by some action that they don't particularly understand, but which causes less harm long-term, apparently, than steroids, and which they try to wean you onto as soon as they can. I had resisted, still thinking that a short course of steroids would cure me, but having been disabused of that notion, I gave in and let him have his way.

I had told him that I totally refused to take Methotrexate, which was what they described as the "gold standard" of DMARDs (disease modifying anti-rheumatic drugs), as the side effects were just too nasty. It's a drug that was developed for cancer patients, but is given to poor unsuspecting arthritics because they have found that it can help... sometimes... before it blows your liver up or blinds you. It's a typical case of hand-me-downs that end up in the rheumatology department, as they still have no idea how to address autoimmunity. Anyway, as I said to Dr. B, I wanted to get rid of my disease, not modify it!

So, among my barrage of various herbal and vitamin pills that I took every morning (most of which were also a total waste of money), there now lurked not only a small dose of steroids, but the two sinister yellow Sulfasalazine pills. I remember I used to swallow them all in one big mouthful, fooling myself that as long as there were more health food shop pills than chemical ones, I was still keeping to my purist view of curing myself naturally.

The Sulfasalazine didn't seem to be having much of an effect until late February when one day I woke up and all was not right with the world by any means. On top of the regular pain I was in a state of abject psychosis. What with the feeling of losing my mind on top of the arthritis, my worst nightmares had come true, and my world totally fell apart.

And then there was the twitching and spasming. This was a whole new experience. As I lay on the sofa my legs and arms would twitch and jump. Sometimes this would happen every couple of seconds on a bad day, but at least several times a minute, and at night it would keep me awake, and Detta too. This was compounded with a sort of "accelerated movement" in that if I reached for anything my hand would seem to leap out of control and perform the action faster or travel further than I intended. I felt like I was not only losing control of my sanity but of my body too.

Even when the psychotic episodes let up for any period of time, there was still awful brain fog. I would shuffle painfully into a room and had no idea why I had gone there. It was a horrible feeling, just how I imagine the start of Alzheimer's would manifest, and when it happened it would trigger a panic attack, which then set off the psychosis again. It was a vicious cycle. I was definitely in trouble, and not having any idea what to do about it was a very lonely, helpless feeling.

⮑ Chapter 2
THE LYME DISEASE FIASCO

I stumbled around the kitchen painfully, joints on fire, trying to remember what I was doing. Thoughts came and went, flitting in and out of the background of pain and panic, but I could seldom hold onto them for long enough to complete a basic task. The acrid smell from the smoking saucepan told me that I had burned my daughter's food. for the second time. This time I just stared at it vacantly. What was happening to me?

"Daddy! Daddy!"

I turned to see Amelia pointing at the sink behind me. In my indecision whether to cook or wash up, I had left the tap running and water was now spraying everywhere from an upturned dish in the sink. It had flooded the floor of the kitchen and soaked my trousers. I hadn't even noticed.

I turned off the cooker and the tap and hobbled into the living room, collapsing on the sofa. My mother appeared around the door and stood there with Amelia, staring at me helplessly. I was supposed to be looking after both of them, but how could I when I could barely look after myself? I just lay there uselessly, joints throbbing, clouded mind racing and my body twitching and vibrating uncontrollably. Surely this was the beginning of the end? How could I come back from this? It felt like every system in my body was on shutdown. It was my very lowest point, and I didn't even have my usual joke or daft comment about it.

I managed to reach for the phone and call Detta at work. "I think you'd better come home…"In the days that followed, I started to research again, but every time I Googled joint pain along with the other symptoms it kept coming up with Lyme disease. Now, I know it's typical hypochondriac behaviour, and

Googling can scare the hell out of you, but no answers were coming from the doctors, so I just had to see what I could put together. Actually, Lyme was not beyond the realms of possibility, as I had clear memories of one tick that I had removed upon returning from a fishing trip, and there's no telling how many others I might have come into contact with and not realised. Also, I had been abroad a lot and been bitten by all sorts, and as I researched it became clear that nobody really had a definitive idea of which insects carry these spirochetes and other nasties that can cause the myriad symptoms of Lyme.

I also learned that it was almost impossible to get a positive diagnosis for Lyme past the first few days/weeks, so doctors would not even be able to treat cases where it had progressed to a dangerous stage. I saw one film in particular full of people twitching and spasming in wheelchairs, facing a slow, agonising and terrifying death while doctors denied they even had Lyme, and that's how I saw my future. The film was made to make people aware of this dreadful disease, as people all over the world were dying while many doctors didn't believe that it was a real condition, and others who did believe were being struck off for going against the guidelines and treating patients, even though they were having success. I was shocked at the mismanagement of what was clearly becoming a worldwide epidemic, of which I suspected I was a victim.

Trying to learn about all of this through a veil of psychosis and brain fog was very difficult, and there were times when I thought that the task in front of me, monumental enough when it was just to cure the arthritis, had now been magnified a thousand times, and I wondered if it was worth it. Regular suicidal thoughts had to be kept at bay. I just had to focus on how much I wanted to see my little girl grow up. Without her I think my story might have ended around 2011.

I also discovered in my research that it was a very bad idea to give either steroids or immunosuppressants to a Lyme patient as it can let all hell loose and hasten in the neurological stage of Lyme, which is exactly what it seemed had happened to me on the steroids and sulfasalazine. Also, in bed one night, I actually felt the inflammation get into my neck in the space of a couple of minutes, and this stiff and painful "Lyme neck", which is what I was left with, is a very common indicator of the disease. It all seemed to add up perfectly.

I did discover a clinic specialising in the treatment of Lyme. In their info on their website it said that they could arrange the more comprehensive Lyme tests only available in the States. This was expensive though, running into thousands, and with still no guarantee of a positive outcome to the test even if infected, and the possibility of repeat tests being necessary it could bankrupt me, and still I'd have no access to the proper treatment. I called them up and spoke to a very knowledgeable lady there who did little to quell my fears about the condition or the possibility of a cure, but she did come out with one line that I didn't really take in at the time, but which in future months I would come to realise was the best bit of advice I could have had. She said, "The first thing we need to do is to heal your leaky gut. If you have been taking medications and have been eating a bad diet for any length of time it's almost certain that you have leaky gut. When that's healed we can see where we are."

I was too focused on my idea that I had Lyme and that it needed some sort of modern medical drug intervention to take heed of her wonderful advice. We are so brainwashed into thinking of having to go straight to a doctor for anything that ails us and put ourselves totally in their hands that it is very difficult to break out of that conditioning and take a more independent course of action. Eventually I would switch paths, but at that time I was on rails and could only go in one direction.

For an idea of how many symptoms can be present in these

autoimmune conditions, and which you might find parallels to in your own history, below is a list of what happened to me over the years, taken from a letter to Dr. B…

MY SYMPTOMS:
Last ten years:
Very intolerant to heat like my 'thermostat' was bust. Redness and flushing (like rosacea but no spots) triggered by the slightest temperature change. Very intolerant to sunlight – seem to have no melanin left. In 2007 investigations into parathyroid for non-specific symptoms came back negative. Same year I had a camera shoved down my throat and told I had hiatus hernia. Lazily, I took Lansoprazole for way too long to combat indigestion. (Cutting out grains has totally sorted that out).

April to June 2010:
Iritis.
Foot pain, which travelled around the right foot.
Rash around midsection, which my GP saw, and which was unresponsive to topical treatment. I have since seen pictures of this exact rash on Lyme patients, which although it was not the classic bullseye, was another very well known form of it.
Severe thoracic spine pain, especially at night.
Frequent low-grade fevers at night.
Extreme fatigue.

June to September 2010:
All the above worsening, plus:
'Rattly' lung when lying on left side (recently also when lying on back).
"Eczema" on hand starting.

October to present:
Both ankles and one knee very swollen and inflamed (at this point I got the reactive arthritis diagnosis).
Resting heart rate of 85-90 (sometimes higher) with palpitations, when it's usually about 70, and even 60 or below when I'm fit.
Depression, mood swings, headaches, nausea, insomnia, short temper.
Most recently – Twitching and spasming muscles in arms and legs, particularly at night.
Stiff and painful neck along with the brain fog.
Anxiety and panic (like adrenaline rushes), dizziness, balance and coordination problems, confusion, unreliable short-term memory, light sensitivity, night sweats.
Muscle wasting in legs.
Slurred speech on a really bad day.
Burning sensations in the hands and wrists under the skin and travelling numbness in fingertips.

To try to get some sort of answer more quickly, I made a private appointment with Dr. B to ask about the possibility of having Lyme. He told me that Lyme disease was not present in the UK above Norfolk, which subsequent research proved to be untrue, and I went home £150 poorer with no useful information at all.

I found evidence of many people up in my area of the UK who were suffering greatly with undiagnosed Lyme, which they had picked up in Cumbria or even further north. I had a brief correspondence with a so-called Lyme expert at a local hospital of rheumatology who kept incorrectly referring to it as "Lyme's disease" and waffled a lot. I just couldn't take him seriously.

The Internet threw up all sorts of insane websites and raving nutters coming up with crazy "cures" for Lyme, which just demonstrated the amount of desperation there is among sufferers. The treatment that came up more often than most was a combination of mega doses of vitamin D along with natural salt and hot baths. I overdosed on vitamin D, taking several grams a day along with Himalayan salt in a glass of water and boiling myself in the bath, desperately looking for evidence of spirochetes leaving the body. I had read questionable accounts of them actually being visible breaking through the skin to escape the hostile environment that the heat, vitamin D and salt created and did get the odd spot and rash as I lay there, but it's hardly surprising – looking back it was probably just burns from the scalding water!

However, I had managed to uncover a few sources of info on genuine natural cures for Lyme, and I was starting to form the first little bud of the idea that there was a chance of beating whatever I had, even if it was Lyme, without the help of doctors at all. When I look back though, it was a significant turning point. I feel so sorry for true Lyme disease patients who cannot even get a diagnosis, let alone treatment.

To cut long story short, I didn't have Lyme, as far as I know, but I touched on the above to demonstrate just how complicated autoimmunity can be in terms of crazy symptoms, sometimes for years before an actual diagnosable disease becomes evident. You can chase round so many departments in the hospital for answers to these problems, but usually you just get puzzled looks from the docs, as they just do not have enough knowledge about autoimmunity to give satisfactory answers.

My advice is that once you know you are autoimmune, do not panic at every little twinge, ache and pain. If you follow the general dietary and environmental advice laid out in part two of this book, the majority of symptoms will vanish anyway, and those that remain will probably be your core issues that you can work on specifically with emotional balancing, also touched upon later in the book.

⊃ Chapter 3
A RAY OF HOPE

At around that time I also got in touch with another rheumatologist, a Dr. S from a specialist hospital of rheumatology nearby. I discussed Lyme with him during a consultation, and I was very encouraged when he didn't dismiss the possibility out of hand like Dr. B had. He actually sat with me and went through pictures of typical rashes on the Internet, one of which I identified as the one I had originally had a couple of months before the joints swelled up. Still, he didn't give me any hope or any solid treatment plan and started banging on about Methotrexate again and how I should start taking it as soon as possible. I explained that I didn't want to go down that route, and he seemed fairly open to me trying natural means, but still, I could see he didn't have any confidence in them. I agreed to X-rays of the affected joints and my spine to aid him in a diagnosis and left with little reassurance.

The one useful thing I got from my association with Dr. S was a diagnosis of psoriatic arthritis. Actually, this is nothing that Dr. B would have missed in the end, as it had gone on more than six months by then, making the initial hopeful diagnosis of reactive arthritis unlikely. He could see from the X-rays that there was some evidence from my sacroiliac joints that it had been with me for a lot longer than I thought, which had probably been the reason I'd had lower back pain so frequently. Also it was clear that the diagnosis of Keinbok's disease in my wrist (a crumbling of the lunate bone due to loss of blood supply) back in the early 90s was probably wrong and that arthritis had been the cause of that pain too. I'm actually glad I never knew what it was back then, because I'd probably have taken more of their nasty drugs, as I'd not have had access to the massive amount of information the Internet has brought with it. Now, I could recount the full story of my experience with Dr. S, but let's just say not only did he prove to be far less open minded than I initially thought, but he actually turned out to be one of the worst doctors I have ever encountered. Having not been able to persuade me to take his pantheon of liver-bursters, he started to get rather aggressive with me, and on one occasion even shouted at me for not taking them, foaming at the corners of the mouth and plying his fear-based nonsense, "But, but, if you don't eventually it will get into your heart!!" He always seemed more interested in berating me for once using his mobile phone number that a receptionist who didn't know the score I suppose, revealed to me unbidden so I could get some X-ray results. However many times I apologised and told him that it was an honest mistake and I didn't obtain the number by nefarious means, he actually called me a liar.

So, there has been enough doom and gloom in the first two chapters, and I'd like to move onto some positivity, but this sort of treatment is extremely common in the NHS when specialists' knowledge is challenged. In the end I actually wrote a letter of complaint to Dr. S and the boss at the hospital describing why I thought his treatment ideas and "bedside manner" were so appalling. I received a reply asking if I'd like to make a formal complaint about him. I didn't; I was far more concerned with getting well, but I did want to make my point. So, in reply to their reply, I wrote my last letter ever to anyone in the NHS and determined to stop looking down that particular blind alley.

Dear ....,

Thank you very much for your reply to my recent letter. However, I have no desire to get Dr S into any trouble so do not wish to make a formal complaint. After all, he hasn't done anything criminal... well, apart from succumbing to the rheumatologists' usual habit of prescribing dangerous chemicals to unsuspecting arthritics who could cure themselves with radical diet and lifestyle changes, but unfortunately that is not regarded as criminal... yet. No, I just wanted to bring to his attention, and to that of the chief executive of the hospital, that Dr S is, to use the medical term, a rude, aggressive, egotistical, closed-minded arse.

Yours,

Phil Escott.

By that April I was still obsessing about being a vegan. I had spent so long doing Transcendental Meditation that I still had the guilt and conditioning around meat that so often comes from such Hindu-based practices. I had been a vegetarian for many years on and off, and when I got ill the guilt came flooding back again, and I had all sorts of strange ideas that the meat I had eaten had somehow caused the problems. I had even written in the first edition of my Pure Activity book that the human digestive system is similar to that of a gorilla. At the time I believed it, but didn't really practice what I preached. Now that things hurt so much I went scurrying straight back to what I had convinced myself was the best diet, and I was living on raw fruit and smoothies.

I had lost about two and a half stone (about 35lbs) since October, which initially seemed like a good thing, but it became clear to me much later that a lot of it was muscle. Worse was the quadriceps muscle on my left leg above the affected knee, which was visibly wasted. I still carried a lot of fat, which covered up much of the muscle wastage. Consequently it went unnoticed, so I was encouraged by the testimony of the bathroom scales and carried on. Although the weight was coming off fast, probably because of ditching the grains, I was still in pain if I ate anything, and I was still bordering on insane. It's no mystery to me now, and I can see that I was on a permanent cycle of sugar rush/crash. I remember it as one of the worst times of the whole episode – surely I was on the right path with the raw diet? But still I was ill. Maybe there really was no way out of this constant pain – maybe the rheumatologists were right and nothing would work. The pain and inflammation made sure that I had to give up all the things I loved doing. I couldn't go night fishing for carp, I couldn't ride a mountain bike properly, only occasionally managing short rides on the road, I certainly couldn't train with weights, and perhaps worst of all, I couldn't play drums. Occasionally I could go to my music room and have a little dabble if my ankles weren't too agonising that day, but there was no way I was ever going to be able to play a gig.

My bandmates had no idea the severity of what was happening to me. They were puzzled, and one was very sympathetic, but the other, who I had considered a great friend for a couple of decades was, let's say, less sympathetic. To be fair, he was facing a lot of his own problems at the time, but in the end, in a flood of animosity, the band broke up. I was so lost in brain fog that I couldn't really grasp what had actually happened until much later, but I did grasp that I had lost one of my major incentives to get well again – playing live music. It was devastating. It would be a long time before I would understand that at such turning points in life many things are taken away, but in the long run they are shed from your life merely to make way for better things. As I hadn't seen the long-term outcome yet, trying to tell myself that at the time was not much consolation.

At my lowest ebb, two events happened that changed my life: Firstly, one day I was Googling around, as I used to do for much of my days and nights in between bouts of fitful sleep on the couch. I was looking for "problems on a raw vegan diet" and came up with a site called "Beyond Vegetarianism". The site was aimed at people who had problems on vegetarian or vegan diets, and it seemed I wasn't on my own by any means. Some had soldiered on for decades, and some had developed problems early on, but the amount of stories of all sorts of health breakdowns made interesting, if depressing reading.

Then I came across a long article written by one of the guys who ran the site, and after an hour or so reading it my jaw was on the floor and my outlook would never be the same again. The article dealt with the confusion caused by following advice given by various diet gurus, all giving out conflicting information. After many years of going from pillar to post of unreliable claims as to what humans should eat, he had ignored all the advice and studied the bone records instead to find out the diet that humans are genetically adapted to.

It was my introduction to the historical fact that once humans grouped together in settlements and started farming, therefore relying on the grains and dairy products that they could not have obtained as hunter-gatherers, the skeletons showed a marked decline in size and health. There was evidence of osteoporosis, teeth were missing, and the height and brain size was in decline. They put forward the theory that humans had evolved while eating meat and fish, to the extent that their habitat had provided it, and that any dogma about vegetarianism was purely based in religious or spiritual practices coming out of the east. We had been meat eaters for millions of years; we were adapted to it, and the reliance on grains, which we had only eaten for about 12,000 years (not nearly enough for a species to adapt genetically) had caused many of the world's chronic disease problems. These same diseases were almost unheard of in present day hunter-gatherer tribes who still ate what nature provided.

Further Googling predictably turned up the exploding craze of the paleo diet and the websites of Mark Sisson and Robb Wolf, who also mentioned even stricter protocols for anyone with an autoimmune condition. The success stories were very encouraging. When I put this together with the information that I had misinterpreted and buried in my brain from Barbara Allen's book and some of the suggestions I had seen in the Lyme disease book I had read, a pattern started to emerge. It still sat a little uncomfortably with my vegetarian mindset, but at last here seemed to be hope.

I remember that very evening just desperately needing a break from my painful, depressing routine and drug abstinence. I took a handful of Paracetamol to get me mobile and headed off to the local Chinese buffet where I ate half my own bodyweight in chicken, duck, pork and beef. I have never enjoyed a meal so much in my life, and the temporary relief I got from the painkillers made it the best day I'd had in a long time. I had a lot to learn about meat quality and the importance of many other aspects of a healing diet, but it was a first step and a delicious one at that. In the weeks that followed, I continued my research with renewed enthusiasm.

The second very significant thing that happened to me was meeting the wonderful Gabi Heyes, a naturopath who came very highly recommended. She ran the Natural Practices clinic not far from where I lived. I spoke to her on the phone and told her of my worries about Lyme and the impossibility of getting a diagnosis, never mind treatment. She was most encouraging, saying that she had had some success already in the treatment of Lyme and that she had a device called a Bio meridian MSAS that diagnosed all sorts of imbalances in the body, including various forms of Lyme disease. She could run me through it and put my mind at rest. It seemed too good to be true, and I could hardly wait to be seen.

She was pretty booked up, but to my delight, and probably because I was clearly in such a panic about Lyme, she offered to see me after her last patient in only a couple of days' time. I could hardly wait. Surely it was too good to be true that I would finally have an answer about the Lyme disease?

The day came for the appointment, and the contrast between

the care and attention I received that evening and what I had been through with the NHS brought a lump to my throat on several occasions. Gabi herself is fun, caring, patient and very knowledgeable. She seemed not only genuinely interested in my rambling tale of woe, listening patiently and carefully with no hint of disapproval or mocking so common with allopathic doctors, but she even had some very useful answers. Encouragingly, she confirmed that yes, there is an end in sight to any chronic disease, and apparently I had already done many useful things from my own research.

Gabi wired me up to her magic machine, and one by one checked all of the balances of vitamins, minerals and so much more in my body. I had been stuffing myself with all sorts of supplements and herbs, still thinking it was all about some magic pill, even if it was a natural one, but it seemed that in my blunderbuss approach I had got a few things right and my vitamin and mineral levels were pretty good. It was a start. However, my liver wasn't working too well, so the natural cycle of ridding the body of toxins had a bit of a blockage, and several other things that I had never even considered were also well out of whack. The machine even detected that I was full of X-rays, and I had indeed that morning gone back to Dr. S for those X-rays of my knee, ankles and back, so that pretty much convinced me that there was something magical going on with Gabi and her device!

It was such a fascinating experience seeing the readings coming up on the computer screen that I almost forgot my Lyme disease panic, but when Gabi ran the tests for various parasites associated with Lyme, my heart started beating a bit faster. However, the reading showed that I didn't have Lyme, and so I vowed at that moment to stop panicking about anything to do with Lyme and just follow my intuition and Gabi's guidelines and support the body in healing itself, trusting that it knew best.

Almost three hours went by in delightful company at that first consultation. I just could not believe how enlivened I felt as I headed out of there with a completely different outlook, a mind boggling list of suggestions for treatment, and best of all a lovely new friend in Gabi who would support me and advise me so generously over the next few years. This is how health care should be! So began my introduction to enemas, castor oil packing, liver flushing and many more all-new treatments to me that would take up hours of my day for a long, long time.

↪ CHAPTER 4
REDISCOVERING MY FATHER

As I mentioned in the first chapter, my father (who had died in 2003 from a heart attack aged 77 after some tremendous NHS over-prescription and delays in correct treatment for a brain tumour) had been diagnosed with rheumatoid arthritis back in the 1950s but had moved to Jordan, and it had disappeared. It now seemed likely that I had inherited the HLA-B27 gene from him and that he had psoriatic arthritis too, not that it was even recognised as a diagnosis back then, as everything was lumped under "rheumatoid". The fact that he also had iritis (I remember him telling a horrified ten-year-old me about his injection in the eyeball, something I would later also experience...) suggested that he was also prone to autoimmunity. He had also had Menier's disease, a condition of the ear, which is also thought to be connected to autoimmunity. So, how did he get better, and how did he have none of the symptoms of any of his previous problems during the last 50 years of his life when it's supposed to be incurable?

I remember thinking as a child that it must have been something to do with moving to a hot climate and the heat loosening up the joints (as everyone complains about joint pain in the winter, don't they?), but of course I didn't understand the process of inflammation, and as the summer of 2011 arrived and I was still suffering, this connection seemed unlikely.

I decided to buy a copy of my father's medical records to see if I could find any more clues. A large pack of papers arrived one day, and I set about poring over them. I was an interesting journey through my father's life, with many of the documents being records of medicals he had undergone for the company he worked for from the 60s onwards, and all of them pretty much gave him a clean bill of health, often specifying that there was no sign of a previous diagnosis of rheumatoid arthritis.

During visits to rheumatologists I had often mentioned the fact that my father had managed to get clear of it when they told me it was incurable, but they always dismissed it, saying that either he had been lucky and it had "burned itself out" or that it was actually a misdiagnosis. Well, taking into consideration the clues of iritis and Menier's it seemed unlikely that it was a mistake.

There were clear records of his visits to the doctor in the early 50s and mention of the barbaric gold injections they subjected him to, and then no records of the disease after he went to Jordan in about 1958. As far as I could work out he had suffered for at least seven years with it, but there was no sign of it in later life, nor was there any lasting joint damage, so again the conventional wisdom was being put under suspicion.

I put myself in his position… He had been living in Bristol with my mother, delivering bread door-to-door on cold winter mornings – a job he hated. I remember him saying that it took him a long time to get moving early in the morning, and he didn't like to stop moving once he did because he would "seize up again", as he put it. He had moved to Jordan to follow his passion; he had always loved and been fascinated with the Middle East, and he wanted to go and help people out there. His main aim was to build orphanages and to care for the many underprivileged children in the region. In the end, as is so often the way, his life took a slightly different course as he met a Dr. Sami Khoury and his young family, who became lifelong friends and are still considered our extended family. He helped Dr. Sami to set up The Palestine Hospital in Amman and even got to know King Hussein and some of his family. He was in his element. My mother moved out there with him, and together they worked in the new hospital when it was set up, only returning (symptom free) to the UK in 1962 when I was on the way. Later he even set up a charity to help Jordanian children with neurological conditions to get free treatment. He really ended up living his dream.

In 2011 I was totally focused on diet and natural remedies for a way out of my own problems, but I know my father would not have bothered with anything like that. Even though his diet probably did change in Jordan, he certainly still ate wheat, which I considered the greatest of all evils, so how did he heal? I could not figure it out at all. At the time I thought I had come to a dead end with my father's story.

Meanwhile, in my own tale, things were looking up. By about June I was a lot more mobile. I had lost a lot of muscle from my raw vegan experiments, and most of the fat had now disappeared from my newfound semi-paleo diet, so I was looking a bit on the thin side, but I certainly felt better. I had now lost about five stone, or 70lbs. I had also been experimenting with fasting, and during those fasts I had enjoyed almost complete remission. I did many fasts, from three to eleven days on water only and came to look forward to them very much. They were like a little holiday from the suffering, and the fact that the symptoms disappeared showed me that it must have some sort of a connection with the digestive system, a fact that the rheumatologists always try to deny.

I found that with just a couple of Paracetamol and/or Ibuprofen (which I used very sparingly due to its dangerous gut-ripping action), I could actually manage to spend one night per week indulging in my beloved carp fishing. I wasn't very strong, and pushing the barrow laden with fishing and sleeping gear around the lake was a struggle and somewhat painful with my inflamed ankles, but it was a tremendous victory for me to no longer be confined to the sofa.

It was during one of these night fishing expeditions that I lay on my bedchair in the bivvy reading a book called "The Healing Code" that had been recommended to me by a very dear friend.

He had reasoned with me that my problems might not all be in the field of diet, but that there must be an emotional root too. I had been what I considered a serious yogi for many years and pompously considered myself above such wooly, sandal-wearing, muesli-knitting practices as delving into your childhood for clues as to why your experiences and emotions might be causing problems years later. However, illness is a great blessing for gradually breaking down all preconceptions and pomposities, and by then I was willing to give anything a go.

That night I read the whole book, and in the morning I began work on the many aspects of one's personality and emotions that the author considered to be potential problem areas. I thought deeply about it all, filled in some forms I had printed out from the website but totally failed to get even the slightest grasp of how it all worked. Looking back I was overcomplicating things so much and digging in all the wrong places (a huge mistake that is so commonplace when new to the idea of emotional balancing) that I shelved it, and it was a couple of years before I found my way back to it properly.

Little did I know at the time, but the answer to why my father recovered was staring me in the face that night. He had followed his dream. He was so unhappy in Bristol, treading water and doing a job that he hated, so the contrast of being in Jordan and doing what he loved and following his ultimate dream had been enough to put him right very quickly. To put it in the words of the wonderful Byron Katie, who I only discovered two years later, in Bristol he was not "loving what is". If you don't love what is for long enough, the body follows suit and starts to attack itself according to your genetics. This I now believe to be the root of autoimmunity.

Also, my father had the added advantage of living in a time when the planet was not so polluted, both with chemicals and with the dreadful electromagnetism that comes from mobile phones and masts and WiFi that disrupts us on a cellular level wherever we go. It was not until I discovered Dr. Jack Kruse a year or so later that I understood why it was far easier to get rid of ailments 50 years ago than it is today. These days we have to go much further into our own biohacks to get answers than my father did all those years ago.

So, in moving to Jordan, my father ended up inadvertently doing exactly what he needed to do to heal. He was lucky. My journey was going to be more complicated.

➲ Chapter 5
GETTING SERIOUS

Throughout 2011 I developed an obsessive daily routine. I'd hole up in the bathroom for hours in the morning indulging in enemas and Epsom salt baths. While doing this I'd generally read some inspiring literature by alternative health experts, healers and medical intuitives like Andreas Moritz or Caroline Myss. I wanted to bolster my confidence that it was actually possible to heal. I could feel the weight of the brainwashing that I'd been given by the medical community, and the rheumatologists in particular, and I wanted rid of it. Such statements as "Diet doesn't make any difference…", "The only thing that works is our pills…" and "Your joints will never be normal again…" are difficult to shift. Any little successes I had were dulled a little by the doubts that had been installed by conventional wisdom.

My morning routine certainly worked though. I'd limp out of the bedroom, but two or three hours later I'd walk out of the bathroom relatively pain-free. Looking back, it was probably the purging of the digestive system that took the inflammation down, because my diet still wasn't perfect, and there was clearly undigested food in there that was causing problems that the enemas cleared out. With all the stress at the time it was more than likely that my magnesium was low too, so Epsom salt baths were certainly a great move.

I was doing a lot of fasting too, as I mentioned in the last chapter, but the real discovery, and what became the highlight of each month for me, was liver flushing. I had heard about a book by Andreas Moritz called "The Amazing Liver and Gallbladder Flush", and to my desperate mind it seemed to hold a lot of answers. I will write more about liver flushing in the second part of this book, but in short, it's a method for supposedly flushing soft intra-hepatic stones, and if you have them, gallstones, from the bile ducts once a month. I ended up doing 34 of them, until my body completely rejected the taste of the food grade Epsom salts used to open the bile ducts before you take a large glass of olive oil to trigger the bile production and expel the stones, and I finally called it a day.

Moritz's theory is that the liver cannot function properly and the body cannot heal while it's clogged up with all sorts of debris that collects there over the years from a bad diet and environmental toxins. Also, the fact that he claimed to have healed rheumatoid arthritis with liver flushing made it all the more relevant to me.

Actually, it did seem to do the trick, and for a few days after each one I did have significantly less inflammation. Whether it was due to the action that Moritz suggested or whether it just gave a thorough wash to the intestines is still debatable, and many think that liver flushing is a hoax, but to me it was a blessed relief.

Around this time, probably after about ten or twelve flushes, I got an appointment to get another ultrasound on my liver, which, a year previously, they had told me was very fatty and contained two cysts. During the scan I asked if it was still fatty, and apparently it wasn't at all. Now, after my dramatic weight loss that's to be expected, but when I asked about the cysts things got a bit more interesting. The lady doing the ultrasound told me that there were no cysts and that it's impossible to get rid of them anyway, so I can't have had them in the first place. I asked her to look at my records to check, and sure enough, the cysts were documented. She looked puzzled, turned me over and over, running the ultrasound over me again and again looking for them, but could not find any. She asked me what I'd done to get rid of them, and I told her about the liver flushing, which I assumed had done the trick, and she said, "Isn't that dangerous?" I laughed and said, "What? Olive oil? And you guys want me to take methotrexate?" It seemed ridiculous to me, and of course the results that day gave me renewed confidence (misplaced or not) in my monthly liver flushes. I even did them fortnightly for a while.

I definitely hadn't nailed the diet yet due to conflicting evidence from the paleo community and the likes of Andreas Moritz who railed against meat and gave me doubts. This resulted in my eating far too much fruit and honey, and my massive avocado, banana and mixed "superfood" smoothies in the mornings could have given an elephant diabetes. I was still weak and in some pain, but just with the removal of all grains and processed food from the diet, I started to shed ailments one by one. Hayfever vanished, my tendency to overheat and flush, which had been the bane of my life for ten years or more calmed right down, and many skin complaints disappeared completely. I was obviously making some headway.

By this time I had given up completely on the NHS and its chemical cop-outs, but I did enjoy my regular visits to Gabi at Natural Practices, and it was very encouraging to see improvement each time in the results from her magic machine. My mineral and vitamin levels were all balancing up, my liver function and its ability to detox was improving all the time, and Gabi was very pleased with my progress.

Back at home, and after my extensive morning routine, I would generally spend most of the rest of the day researching on the Internet about all aspects of diet and healing. I discovered so many wonderful and not so wonderful websites leading me down all sorts of rabbit holes of knowledge, but they all seemed to lead back in some way to paleo principles. Eating like a caveman, or at least as close as we can get in this modern age, seemed to be turning round more illnesses than other methods, and more previously conventional doctors seemed to be coming over to this way of thinking and had started writing about it. I still had a way to go to get rid of my vegetarian principles and my adherence to the misinterpreted Ayurvedic theories that my time in the UK Transcendental Meditation movement had left me with. I was eating meat, but with some guilt, and definitely mixing it with too many (albeit natural) sugars.

I started to get the idea that it wasn't just diet that affected us. It was clear that our food is not the only thing that has changed in the past few centuries, and we looked at many aspects of our environment. A big one was getting somebody in to test for EMFs in the house. After a thorough going over with his EMF meters, it became clear that we were living in an EMF nightmare. The music/rehearsal room, which doubled as my study, was the worst. We had so many electronic gadgets, lighting and computers in there that it's hardly surprising it had contributed to my declining health, as I spent most of the day in there.

We made a lot of changes. We got rid of WiFi, and even more harmful, the devices that boost its signal by routing it through the mains electricity. We had these devices in the bedroom, plugged in right by our heads, and their removal alone resulted in a significant improvement in sleep for my daughter and my partner, and the abrupt end of the regular headaches she was waking up with.

We also fitted blackout blinds in the bedroom and bought earthing sheets to sleep on and earthing pads to use while at the computer. These are cotton sheets woven through with conductive metal that plug into the earth socket, or, much better, straight into the ground outside via a copper rod to "earth" the body and hopefully discharge any buildup of electromagnetism. They also seemed to help with sleep, and I noticed that not only did they seem to reduce inflammation, but the regular electric shocks that Detta and I used to get from each other and from car doors etc became a thing of the past. I also used to spend as much time barefoot in the garden as I could, and this definitely had an instant effect on inflammation too.

It took a lot to keep the inflammation down, and my lifestyle became rather restrictive, but at least all the methods added up were working. I was aware that it was still just symptom control though, and it seemed as though I was trying to plug hundreds of holes in a sinking ship's hull with only ten fingers. I still felt overwhelmed on a regular basis.

Despite this confusion and slow progress, I decided I was well enough to organise a family holiday in Thailand at a fishing resort owned by a good friend and his family. I had been once before in 2010, maybe a month before I got really ill, and this time, in January 2012, I returned a shadow of my former self. By now about 75lbs lighter, I could see in the family's faces that they had some concerns about me, having not seen me for 16 months. I also had my doubts that my weakened body was up to battling with the monsters living in the lake, but in the end I proved up to the task, landing huge stingrays, Siamese carp, Mekong catfish and even an arapaima of double my own bodyweight, but it was not without some considerable pain.

Although I was eating one good paleo meal a day of some meat, fat and veg, I did tend to start the day off with a bucket full of mangoes and bananas, so I am not surprised looking back that there were occasions where I hobbled round the lake in the morning to start to fish. Actually I had some very low times on that holiday. I remember a couple of nights sobbing with agony and despair while Detta lovingly massaged my swollen ankles as I fell asleep, tormented by the hopeless depression that I might never get better. Being on that holiday magnified the perception of just how ill I had got since I had last visited, so it blocked out awareness of any progress I had made since I could barely even walk a year previously. Of course, like anyone would be, I was impatient to see the back of it.

Upon my return to the UK I continued my research and made perhaps my two most important discoveries in the field of diet: the doctors Jack Kruse and Natasha Campbell McBride. They are both neurosurgeons whose paths have veered somewhat from the conventional. McBride cured her own son of autism by addressing his diet, and Kruse reversed his own obesity and other issues. Independent of each other they took a similar route, that of a low carb ketogenic diet, high in fat and utilising bone broths and fermented foods as probiotics to heal the gut and balance the gut flora. Jack Kruse also stresses the importance of DHA from fish in what he calls his Epi-Paleo Rx. Natasha Campbell McBride's approach is called "GAPS" or Gut and Psychology Syndrome, and her dietary recommendations have become known as the GAPS diet.

As I immersed myself in their websites and YouTube talks I really felt that I was starting to get somewhere. Everything they said made total sense, and one particular video of McBride on YouTube called "Wise Traditions London 2010" made me feel like I had just been given the key to the human immune system and why it gets confused as the gut flora breaks down. She covers everything from ADD to autism and on the autoimmunity side, everything from arthritis to asthma. Jack Kruse's website is harder work, but the science is so deep on there that it gave me great confidence that he knew what he was talking about. He also delved far more into the environmental mismatches we have invented since we were hunter-gatherers and how this reflects in the physiology, causing all sorts of modern, or as he puts it, Neolithic diseases.

It made perfect sense that the way out of these recent epidemics of chronic diseases lay in removing the stresses that didn't exist before they started. I began to focus on subtraction rather than addition in my approach to regaining my health, and my confidence soared. I finished up the last batch of what were probably mostly useless supplements and resolved not to buy any again unless I had a pretty clear idea that I actually needed them. The blunderbuss approach I had taken to supplementing during the previous year had probably cost me enough to buy a decent car. Knowing what I know now, that nutrition is more a case of efficiency of absorption (which is down to healthy gut flora) than massive vitamin and mineral dosing, I wouldn't have bothered in the first place and probably wouldn't own such a crap car as I do now, at the time of writing.

I began to understand about the dangers of even natural sugars and eating too much fruit and started to veer towards a very low carb ketogenic diet. It felt good, and the sugar cravings soon died down. On the upside, I felt a lot better, and the inflammation retreated even more, but I did start to lose even more weight. It became clear to me that I had lost most of the muscle on my raw vegan trip a year previously, and now as the low carb diet melted the last of the fat I looked like a prisoner of war.

Also, this low level of body fat allowed me to notice that I had also developed an inguinal hernia. It's hard to say how long it had been there, but a visit to the surgeon revealed that I needed an operation. Now, I was getting a bit cocky with my ability to heal anything that I declined and said I would try to do it myself. More research began, and I found a few websites giving techniques and exercises for healing hernias without surgery. I was annoyed that I had yet another health issue to deal with, but stoically rose to the challenge, and ploughed on confidently.

Then I hit a setback. One day while having lunch in a restaurant in Manchester, I filled the urinal with blood. It certainly spoiled my meal, and anyone who has ever passed blood will confirm that it's a worrying experience. I returned to my table and told Detta. Predictably when I got home and started consulting "Dr. Google" things went from bad to worse as I decided I'd got everything from bladder cancer to advanced kidney disease. It made the hernia problem seem very small.

To cut a long, boring story short, I went for the tests – a camera down the urethra to check the bladder wall for problems and I had an ultrasound for kidney stones. Both came back negative, so I started imagining that I had destroyed my kidneys with painkillers and anti-inflammatories and that I was as good as dead.

I had an appointment to see a specialist and he didn't do much to quell my fears, introducing the possibility of kidney cancer too. He organised a scan for me and in the meantime I decided to do a long fast in an effort to reverse anything that had gone wrong. At the time I was convinced that fasting was the answer to everything, and what I really wanted to do was a 40-day water only fast, as I had seen evidence that fasts of that length had at times reversed almost anything. However, with my bodyweight and muscle mass so low I didn't feel I had the reserves for it, and if my memory serves me right, I made it to eleven days.

Apart from the worries about my collapsing kidneys, those eleven days were heaven. Get that far into a fast and all inflammation disappears. I felt light, energetic and totally pain-free. Not only that, but the blood disappeared from my urine. I spent the time researching more into the GAPS diet and resolved that when I broke my fast I would give it a proper go. I had high hopes that this was the turning point. If I came out of the fast and didn't eat any carbs, surely this would mark the end of my journey? At last I had a solid plan. What could possibly go wrong?

On the day I broke my fast I remember cooking some chicken and sitting on a rug in the garden to eat it. Of course my stomach was small after the fasting, so it didn't take long to feel full. I got up to relieve myself and was horrified to find that my ankles had inflamed in just the short time since I had eaten. I hobbled to the toilet, dismayed enough, but when that familiar bright red stream hit the water in the pan, I was devastated. Not only could I not seem to eat anything if I wanted to be pain free, but since I had bled again after the chicken, the kidneys were probably worse than I had expected, as they could take no protein any more. Never have I experienced such a downturn in mood in such a short time in my life. I was now pretty scared.

I even remember sitting down and writing a desperate email to Natasha Campbell McBride asking her advice on adapting the GAPS diet for those with bad kidney function. Needless to say she never did reply to my ramblings.

Looking back I can see exactly what happened. Chicken can be corn fed and can be quite a spectacular trigger for arthritis. It certainly isn't the best meat if you have autoimmune issues. Also, the bleeding starting again was probably not even connected to what I had eaten given my subsequent diagnosis, but the combination of disasters that day definitely set me back, as it ruined my confidence in what eventually proved to be the ideal course of action for me, and it sent me back to my morning sugary smoothies for a while, as I really believed the nonsense that protein is bad for the kidneys.

Finally my scan date came around, and I was to be found lecturing the rather overweight radiographer about the paleo diet as I was loaded into the machine. I was nothing if not persistent in those days! Although he wouldn't tell me what was actually wrong, he was nice enough to set my mind at rest and say in confidence that it didn't look like anything serious. Somewhat relieved, I waited for my appointment with the consultant again for clarification.

When the appointment came around I was told that I had a kidney stone, which for some reason hadn't shown up on the earlier ultrasound. I felt so daft for being so worried, but also slightly annoyed that the oversight of whoever had scanned me had resulted in all these worries. If I had known that I had a stone I would have taken very different measures. However, it was quite substantial, I was told, at 6x4mm, and the doc advised me to get it broken up with ultrasound as it had moved to near the entrance to the ureter where it was rattling round causing bleeding, and it might cause problems due to being around the upper size limit to be able to pass on its own.

There followed a lot of research into ways to dissolve stones, and I came across a book that recommended a fast on apple juice plus other ingredients, saying confidently that it would dissolve any stone. I spent ages juicing the tons of apples needed to last the required 48 hours. By the second day of drinking this amount of sugar, my joints were inflamed and in agony, but I pressed on, seriously believing that it was worth it to shift the stone. I very much doubt that it did any good.

That summer I visited my son Tom who was staying in Granada in Spain for a year as part of his languages course at university. I had felt the kidney stone grumbling on the plane out there, and hoped that it wouldn't attack properly until I got home. One day I agreed to drive Tom and a couple of his friends to Nerja on the coast to do some rock climbing on the beach.

One of his friends was a young lady who was a student doctor back in the UK. I remember chatting with her about health and the misconceptions that the NHS have about a healthy diet. It was all going okay until I mentioned that there was never anything wrong with saturated fats and cholesterol in the diet, and it was all a total misconception that they caused heart disease. She was so annoyed at this challenge to the conventional "wisdom" that she actually told me to shut up, as she couldn't accept that nonsense and was too annoyed to discuss it any more.

We fell into silence, unlike my kidney stone, which chose that exact moment to move into the entrance of the ureter, and I was suddenly in screaming agony. There was nothing for it; I just had to bear the pain and drive everyone back to Granada, as nobody else was insured for the car. I had no painkillers, so it was perhaps the longest two hours of my life. I have no idea to this day how I managed it.

Back at my son's flat I took a cold shower, and to my surprise the pain vanished. I remember peeing hopefully, looking out for the stone as it passed out of the bladder, but there was no sign. After about 15 minutes the pain returned, so it was clear it was still stuck. It was an interesting example of the power of the cold on bodily systems though, and a little taste of my later adventures with cold thermogenesis.

After about four rounds of cold showers, I just could not take the pain any more, and my son walked me to the hospital, which was fortunately just around the corner. My mind could not grasp much at all beyond the pain, but it did occur to me that it was now quite late at night, and I had a flight back to the UK early in the morning. I wondered how I was going to make it.

My son, fluent in Spanish, explained my predicament while I writhed on the reception counter, all dignity gone. At the time I'd have taken anything to get rid of the pain; even cyanide would have been welcome. Anyway, they dosed me up and took an X-ray – not the best way to locate a kidney stone, but it was all that was available on the spot. As the medication kicked in, I waited in bliss in the waiting room, grinning like an idiot that the pain had gone. The doctor called me in to say that he agreed with me that it was a stone, but they couldn't see much on the X-ray. It looked like there was something in the vicinity of the ureter, but it might be something else, as it looked far too big to be the stone I had described. Puzzled, I returned to my son's flat, totally spaced out on the medication, and I slept fitfully until dawn.

I woke up pain-free, so I decided to risk the flight home. It all went well, and back in England I had another scan, which revealed that yes, the stone was stuck half way down the ureter, but it was now 11x8mm and very unlikely to pass on its own. The only option now was to have it broken up by putting a laser into the urethra, through the bladder and into the ureter under general anaesthetic and blasting it to bits. I could not understand why such a massive stone stuck in the ureter wasn't causing tremendous pain, but the body is nothing if not adaptable, and it only grumbled a little every few days.

The surgeon who was going to do the operation advised me to take a course of antibiotics to prevent the awful infections possible when a stone is stuck for a prolonged period of time, but I declined. I had spent too long healing my gut and replenishing the good bacteria to risk wiping it out again with antibiotics. Again I was faced with a doctor who thought I was insane, but I drank a lot of water and took a lot of D-Mannose sugar, which is a sugar that isn't metabolised but does wonders for keeping the urinary tract clear by flushing out the E. Coli bacteria predominantly responsible for problems there. It worked, and there was never any sign of infection.

Meanwhile though, I was facing the operation for the inguinal hernia. I was totally sick of the ridiculous underpants I'd acquired with hard pads to keep hernias in place. They made my nether regions boil up, and I am surprised my sex life survived considering how stupid they looked. Detta is a patient and understanding woman. One plus side to being so skinny was that the doctor said it would be far easier to operate. It all went well, and I returned home to recuperate. However, I was developing some significant palpitations and misfires in my heart, but didn't pay too much attention to them. I had so many odd symptoms, and by this time I was sick of being frightened about every little thing that happened. I had learned my lesson with the unfounded kidney damage panic, and I was starting to trust the body that it knew what it was doing.

Not long after I had recovered from the hernia surgery, I was back in again for the kidney stone to be lasered. Again, all went well, and I spent a satisfying couple of days peeing out the shards of the offending rock, blood and bubbles of air – an odd experience. The good news was that it didn't seem to have damaged the ureter at all, and to the surgeon's surprise he didn't even need to put a stent in to keep the tube clear as it healed. Perhaps my routine of lots of liquids, herbs and D-Mannose had worked. I felt drained by the two operations when my body was at such a low ebb already, but I relaxed knowing that I'd been through the worst, and my healing path was back in my own hands again.

A couple of weeks after that op, I went into the local town with Detta and Amelia to do some shopping. My heart had been misfiring more than usual as we walked around, but then, while standing in the health food shop, it just became too alarming, missing every third beat and "stalling", and I told Detta that I felt I should go to hospital to get it checked.

Having taken an ECG, the local hospital seemed to take my situation rather seriously. They sprayed stuff under my tongue and sent me in an ambulance to another hospital that was better equipped. It's the first time I ever saw Detta actually look worried, and since she was a nurse herself, this worried me too.

Tests showed it was more of an electrical problem, and after a night under observation and awful fluorescent lights, I was told that despite how alarming the symptoms were, it was not the sort of arrhythmia that was likely to kill me any time soon, and I could go home. A week or so later I had an ultrasound of the heart and a 24-hour monitor to catch the patterns of the misfires.

While I waited for the test results, some delving into Jack Kruse's website came up trumps again, and I learned about general anaesthetic very often causing a lot of stress in the body, thereby depleting magnesium significantly. I'd had two in a row, so it was likely that it was at least a contributing factor. Over the next few days I piled in the magnesium malate supplements and took Epsom salt baths. This calmed down the heart considerably and the panic also subsided a little. Still, I was starting to doubt my massive intake of saturated fat. The brainwashing goes deep, and even though I had lost a ton of weight by swapping carbs for fats, I was now wondering if I had damaged my heart by my indulgence in fatty foods.

About a week later I got a phone call from the head cardiologist. The conversation went something like this:

Me: "Go on then... What have I got?"

Doc: "Well, your heart looks strong to me. No issues at all physically. All the arteries clear and a good strong heartbeat."

Me: "Okay, so what's causing the misfires? I have been taking a lot of magnesium and it seems to have calmed it down."

Doc: "Great idea. Five years ago I'd probably have put you on beta-blockers, but I don't think there's any need. What you have is not dangerous and might disappear completely, or it might come and go and you might have to learn to live with it, but don't worry about it."

Me: "Okay, so you say my heart and arteries are clear. Is this the heart of a 50-year-old guy who lives on saturated fat?"

I was spoiling for a fight and expected a lecture, but there was just a pause, and then...

Doc: "We know..."

Me: "What?"

Doc: "We know... well, a lot of us do, that the high fibre/low fat diet that's been touted for the past few decades is a load of rubbish and rather dangerous, but how do we tell people that out of the blue? We'd get lynched! I try to tell people as and when I can... But you carry on with what you're doing. It's perfectly safe."

I was stunned. After all the negativity I'd had to endure from closed-minded rheumatologists, it was a revelation. I had taken the call thinking the path I had taken was wrong and that I was about to be told I was going to die. Instead, I learned that my heart was fine, the way I was going about eating and healing was perfectly safe, and I'd had my faith in the medical profession significantly restored. I remember going back into the living room to tell Detta and punching the air with delight. It was an important moment for me and for my confidence.

As an afterthought on the heart business, I managed to calm the misfires down to just the occasional blip here and there in the day. But then my son found the answer. While researching for a health issue of his own he came across the idea to drink a quarter to half a teaspoonful of Himalayan salt in some water first thing in the morning to further balance electrolytes and aid with hydration. He pointed out that while eating a very low carb diet it is even more essential to address electrolytes and that the body's requirement for sodium goes up considerably. Even to me, this seemed very unlikely to have any real effect, but having nothing to lose I gave it a go. To my enormous surprise, it completely resolved any palpitations, and I have since seen this simple little fix work wonders with many issues that people have run into while adapting to a low carb diet.

After that chat with the cardiologist I didn't feel the need to consult a doctor again. It was a great sense of liberation. I was excited that I was responsible for my own healing again.

⊃ **Chapter 6**
BEYOND DIET AND INTO THE COLD

When you have an autoimmune condition, it doesn't just confine itself to the parts of the body that are primarily affected, such as the joints in arthritis. All sorts of systems can be knocked out as little patches of inflammation burn here and there like scattered bush fires. If you take too much notice of them, they will drive you mad, sending you from department to department in the health system, searching for a diagnosis for every little thing. Eventually I realised that it's all a matter of reducing systemic inflammation and then seeing what you are left with. A low carb diet had helped to reduce the symptoms so much, but they were still grumbling away, and later on in 2012 I started to look seriously at methods outside of diet.

I was still not sleeping very well. Sometimes it seemed as though I would wake up every few minutes, or if I were lucky I'd get an hour in here and there. I knew that unless I got it sorted, I'd be unlikely to heal completely since most of the body's repair mechanisms kick in when we are asleep.

Again, the Jack Kruse's website had a lot to offer. Two things caught my attention: his cold thermogenesis (CT) protocol and cutting out blue light after sundown to maximise melatonin production. I will go into detail about these in the second part of this book, but briefly, if you chill the skin down with cold baths etc it can reduce systemic inflammation in the same way as putting a bag of frozen peas or ice on a sprained joint can help. Also, if you cut out blue light from light bulbs, TVs, computer screens etc before you go to bed, it allows the receptors in the eyes to trigger melatonin production, which is the key to a good night's sleep. One day I decided that it was time to give it a proper go. I was a little apprehensive because nobody likes a cold bath, and at the time I was very thin so there wasn't much insulation. In my excitement I decided to bypass Jack Kruse's safety recommendations of easing into CT via face dunking and ice packs on the chest and ran myself a very cold bath and got straight in. The shock was horrible, but after a minute or so it was replaced with a kind of warm glow, which wasn't too bad at all. After maybe five minutes I began to shiver, so I got out again. The shivering went on for quite some time, and I couldn't seem to warm up my skinny body for the whole evening.

I also put on some orange tinted sunglasses to cut out the blue light while I waited for bedtime, which wasn't long, as I was surprisingly tired despite my teeth chattering. I was thinking that since I was that cold I would never be able to fall asleep, and began to doubt the validity of Dr. Kruse's ideas. Sometime later, still too cold to relax, I got into bed, preparing myself for a worse night than usual. Imagine my surprise then when I woke up a full eleven hours later, in exactly the same position I'd fallen asleep in. I felt amazing – rejuvenated – and at that moment I really knew Jack Kruse was onto something.

Over the next few months I took regular cold baths and face dunks. Sometimes when my ankles were inflamed, a cold bath would completely take away the inflammation within ten minutes, and I'd skip nimbly out of the bathroom, so relieved. A side effect of the cold baths was something else that Jack Kruse had written about – it completely wiped out even the small amount of fat that I had left. As I looked down at my not only lean, but now actually ripped body, I had difficulty believing it was mine. After all, I had spent the last couple of decades with at least a moderate covering of fat no matter how much exercise I'd done. Now, with zero exercise and a ketogenic diet plus regular CT, and I had turned into a walking anatomical diagram.

Soon I was able to extend my time in the cold baths. As winter approached the tap water got even colder, and at times I would supplement it with ice cubes. The first time I got into a cold bath I shivered at about five minutes, but after a couple of months I was starting to get "cold adapted" and could stay in for 15 or 20 minutes before shivering. I started to get rather obsessed with the cold, and when the snow arrived I used to love going out for walks around the garden with no top on, and even tried to adapt my bare feet to be able to walk on it. This is easier said than done.

That winter was a huge turning point for me. Although I still had some pain in my joints, particularly my ankles, I had discovered many ways to control that pain, and I was starting to get reasonably mobile. Pretty much all of my other, lesser symptoms had by now disappeared. I had no twitching or spasming, I was sleeping well, all my skin conditions had disappeared, and my digestion was coming back on line. I started to phase out my morning enema routine, and the last one I ever did also contained a probiotic in an attempt to replace any of the good bacteria I suspected I might have washed out with my hundreds of enemas over the previous two years. I remember it having a rather dramatic effect, and I have not felt the need to do an enema of any type since. Although my body was skinny and weak, it felt to me like I had finished the demolition stage of the rebuilding process. The worst was over.

As I mentioned in the first chapter, at the time we were living in a big three-storey house with my 90-year-old mother. She had the middle floor and we had the ground floor and the top floor. All her life she had been quite a difficult character, and now with no friends and family left apart from us, and me being an only child, it fell on us to look after her. Much as I loved her, nobody on the planet had the ability to make me as angry as she did, and her constant criticism and disapproval chipped away at me. She had suffered a stroke in 1996, which affected her speech, and since then she had completely given up on looking after herself. She washed herself and did her own laundry, but she decided to rely on others for shopping, cooking, etc. Detta had lived with us since 2006, and she really has the patience of a saint, but by the end of 2012, she was ready to shoot my mother too! I used to joke that if my mother was locked in a room with Gandhi for an hour he'd probably end up punching her.

I had felt really trapped for a long time, and at one stage I remember reading, I think in a book by Andreas Moritz, that if your ankles are giving you trouble, look for what it is that you are trying not to run away from. Even though I had not really managed to figure out what my emotional issues were yet, it was obvious that my relationship with my mother was a huge contributing factor to any stress I was piling upon myself. Although nothing she did was particularly bad in isolation, the constant disapproval and criticism took its toll. I used to try to change my attitude to her with EFT and other emotional balancing techniques, and although it helped a little and stopped me blaming her so much, it was still only an intellectual victory. I didn't know how to unlock the emotions and false beliefs at their source.

We had wanted to move house for some time, but we had been delayed by difficulties selling it, and by the fact that I probably wasn't well enough yet anyway, so we shelved the idea. Around Christmas 2012 we put the house back on the market and got an offer on it very quickly. We moved into a rental house early in 2013, and I found a nice little flat nearby for my mother. Even though we had always had our differences, it was a sad day when we waved goodbye to her in her new home for the first time. Even Detta shed some tears. It was clear that I was actually very close to her, or I wouldn't have cared so much to either have been sad or to have felt such strong negative feelings towards her, but I have to admit it was a relief when we spent the first night on our own, knowing that her influence was no longer under the same roof.

Then, over the next couple of months, a miracle happened. Almost as soon as we moved, I noticed a marked improvement in my ankles, and soon enough they seemed to have healed. I still had some problems with my left knee and my right wrist, but the very worst of my symptoms had always been in my ankles. Yet now, with no other lifestyle changes apart from moving away from my mother, all the inflammation died down, and the visibly swollen tissues went back to normal. After about three months I found it hard to imagine that there had ever been anything wrong with them. It was such a wonderful relief, and a massive clue for me that it was not all about diet, but there were some subtler, deeper issues at play here. However, as mentioned, I still had problems with other joints, so the arthritis was still active, but any rheumatologist will tell you that it's impossible to completely cure one joint while others are still inflamed. It was a huge victory for me and another one of my most significant turning points.

My halfhearted attempts at looking at the emotional issues had been stalled because of lack of confidence. Although I had been a hippy and a yogi in my time, when the shit hits the fan and you're really ill, it's suddenly much harder to have confidence in subtler methods of healing. But now, having moved away from my mother and having seen my ankles completely heal up, it gave me the huge confidence boost I needed to really start looking into other issues. I started to tap (EFT) sometimes hundreds of times per day, which is really how dedicated you have to be to get results. Also around the same time I came upon Byron Katie's "The Work", which was huge in my discovery of myself... but I will write more about that and the absolute miracle it led me into in the third part of the book, so enough about it for now.

Throughout the spring and summer I continued to experiment with food, honing the ketogenic diet and finding exactly what my triggers were. It's funny, but although there are some wonderful guidelines about food for autoimmunity out there, everyone is different, and it can take years to really figure out how you are affected by which foods and in what combinations, and even by the time of day they are consumed. It was a long, laborious puzzle, but at least now I probably know more about my body's reaction to foods than almost anybody.

One other experiment I did on myself probably warrants a mention here. Although I had read people like Jack Kruse and Dr. Mercola writing about distilled water not being such a good idea to drink, I decided to give it a go. I had discovered several sources where the virtues of distilled water were extensively hyped. Apparently, not only did it cure every ailment under the sun, but its chelating action stripped the body of all toxins including heavy metals, and decalcified the pineal gland to allow the development of higher states of consciousness. How could I ignore that?

I didn't muck about; I bought a £1500 distiller capable of producing three gallons per day and drank it exclusively... at least one gallon per day. Everything seemed to go okay until about five months in when I started to lose my sense of taste. Pretty soon I couldn't taste anything at all. In fact it was worse than that: I was left with a totally inexplicable sort of "negative" taste, a horrible experience every time I took a mouthful. Eating became an ordeal, and since I was still only about 125lbs I was getting worried that I wouldn't be able to eat enough to maintain any bodyweight at all and I'd fade away.

Dr. Google suggested that given the loss of taste, I had either Bell's palsy, a brain tumour or a severe zinc deficiency. I thought the first two unlikely, and a home test kit for zinc deficiency showed that it was probably the case. I started to pile in the zinc supplements, and gradually over the next two months my sense of taste came back. It was an alarming lesson. Maybe the distilled water did some good and stripped a lot of bad stuff too; maybe I should have stopped at three months as some people recommended. I suppose that there is even a small chance that it wasn't even the cause of the loss of taste in the first place, as some fans of it still claim when I tell them, but it does seem likely that it was, since several sources warn of it stripping the body of good stuff as well as bad stuff.

So, lesson learned, I sold my big, shiny distiller at a massive loss to a local dentist for sterilising his equipment, which is what it should have been used for in the first place. At least we now had some work surface back in the kitchen. The damn thing took up half the room!

So, with my health improving, I looked to getting back to some of my regular activities. I had written a novel, An Illusion of Maya, ten years previously, and had recently had it published. It is about travels in India, a Bedouin past life, soulmates, some naughty bits, and, oddly, long session carp fishing. The last element had attracted the attention of a publisher who usually published out-and-out fishing books, so I got to spend some time that year at the carp fishing shows, signing my book. For the first time in a long time I felt some sense of purpose not connected simply with healing my body.

Being at the carp shows also gave a taste for getting back into fishing again, and I managed to get out for a night every week without actually having to take painkillers. The sense of freedom and independence was exhilarating. It's amazing what we take for granted and only value when we lose the ability to do it.

Still, getting back to my first love, music, seemed a long way off. I remember when I was very ill listening to a discussion between a few of the so-called health gurus in which they were asked what they thought was the number one factor for ensuring good health. David "Avocado" Wolff's reply had stuck with me. He said that by far the most important thing, way ahead of diet or anything else, was doing what you loved – following your heart. Not doing so created a permanent state of not loving what is and kicking against your life situation, so it was bound to eventually result in ill health. But I was still so weak, and having lost both my band and the friendship of my main musical collaborator in bizarre circumstances, I could not imagine how I was ever going to get back into drumming.

At this point fate played a lovely hand in the form of running into a good friend of mine at the local shops. He said he was forming a band and asked if I would like to play drums. My first reaction was to decline on the grounds that I really didn't think I was up to it, and I also doubted that my wrist would put up with holding a drumstick, let alone actually hitting anything with it. However, something told me to just accept and worry about the logistics later on. After all, the band was still in its rehearsal stage, so I wouldn't be required to play any gigs straight away. If it didn't work out at least I would have tried.

Soon after, the same friend asked me to go to a party where some people he knew were playing. It was my introduction to the local blues scene and all the wonderful characters involved in it. I was asked to sit in and play one tune with the band, and although I was far from my best, I did manage to hold my own pretty well, and it felt marvellous to find out I could actually do it.

This led on to playing at many open mic nights where I was welcomed with open arms into the scene by some of the loveliest, most open, ego-free musicians I had ever met. It was a breath of fresh air to be back on acoustic drums with space to improvise after the electronic restrictions of my previous band, and the wonderful vibe of the musicians at these events made me realise that what I thought were good musical relationships beforehand were nothing of the sort. I was soon being asked to play proper gigs with a variety of different incredibly talented musicians, some of whom have become very dear friends and whose bands I still play in at the time of writing. I'd like to say a very big thank-you to them all for pretty much saving my life and bringing me back from the dead.

Being able to play again gave me a huge boost in my confidence and happiness, and this soon reflected in my physiology as the inflammation died down even more. Although I was still incredibly skinny and had to wear a neoprene support strap on my wrist to allow me to play, I was getting stronger and stronger day by day. I could not believe how far I had come, and all those months of strict diet and daily routine were starting to pay off. I was out of the woods.

For a long time I had known about low dose naltrexone (LDN), an old, established and safe drug that was said to be able to switch off autoimmune conditions, although that wasn't its original purpose. It was invented to block the opiate receptors in addicts to help them to come off their drugs. I had always resisted taking it, as I wanted to do it all on my own, but kept it in the back of my mind as a plan B if my own efforts failed. Now however, having tasted success, I was getting impatient to get to the "finishing line" and get rid of the niggling wrist and knee problems, allowing me to play some comfortable gigs, so I decided this was the time to finally try it. Anyway, it is so popular these days as an alternative to the awful chemicals the mainstream doctors and drug companies want to fill you with that I knew I'd have to try it at some point, if only to be able to write about it from personal experience in this book. I got myself a supply, and although I would not say it's the miracle it's made out to be, it did take the symptoms down a notch or two again, so gigs became even more enjoyable. I will go into detail about LDN in the next part of the book.

The result was that by the autumn I was able to play drums

without discomfort, and best of all, I could start to reintroduce some foods that previously hurt me, notably dairy. High fat dairy like ghee, butter, cream and hard cheeses should not be a problem to most people, but they are best given up while trying to heal the gut. Having even had a problem with the safest two, ghee and butter, over the previous two years I could now indulge in masses of cheese and heavy cream. It was heaven! I had missed it so much and most days wolfed a large hunk of cheese and maybe a whole carton of double cream over some berries. I never missed bread, rice and pasta and all the stodgy stuff, but giving up cheese and cream was difficult.

I was also able to start weight training again. When I had owned and run my own gym back in the late 90s I had some spectacular success with abbreviated routines both for myself and for the people I was training. Just using a few basic multi-joint exercises and going heavy on them seemed to be so much more effective than messing around with all the fiddly little isolation exercises that most people opted for. It was a brutal way to train, but it got results. I knew I couldn't train anywhere near as heavy as I used to, so I cast around for a way to train effectively but not have to go so heavy until the joints really came back on line.

The solution came in the form of a book called "Body by Science" by Doug McGuff, a US Emergency Room doctor who was also well versed in paleo and low carb diets. He advocated super slow reps with much lighter weights, but still training very few exercises and very infrequently, but going well into muscular failure on each set. It wasn't new information to me, but it was so well explained that it inspired me to try. I began on these routines, and to my surprise grew my muscle back very quickly. By the spring of 2014 I had put on what I estimate to be about 25lbs of muscle, and I felt so much stronger and healthier. This was from only about ten or twelve minutes of actual training twice a week or sometimes even twice every ten days. Okay, I had built muscle previously, so it's always easier second time around, but it was still a remarkable accomplishment.

Having felt a bit starved for the previous couple of years, my massive intake of cheese and cream also brought with it some fat, and I lost my abs, particularly since I was well out of ketosis by then and was also using the occasional sweet potato (and very occasional white potato) to fuel my workouts. This was not helped by the reintroduction of red wine too, which must have been unbalancing my insulin to some extent, but what the hell? I was having fun. It felt wonderful after being so strict, and unless I ate nightshades two days in a row, my joints didn't give more than a slight hint that they were ever affected.

I also got into HIIT, or "high intensity interval training". In the previous spring of 2013 just after we had moved house, I remember one morning going out mountain biking. I could barely get to the end of the street, let alone get to the off-road trail I had intended on enjoying. It was a bit shocking, and it actually put me off riding for most of the year. However, the following winter, alongside the abbreviated weight training I was doing, I also did a few sprints with a mountain bike mounted in a turbo trainer, amounting to only about eight minutes twice a week including five all-out efforts and a warm-up and cool down. When I went out on the bike for real in the next spring of 2014 for the first time for ages, I rode for half the day and could barely tire myself out. Even to me it was stunning what HIIT had done over the winter. Could it really have even had such a dramatic effect on my endurance capacity too? It seems so…

So that's the physical side of my story really. The improvements continued for another year or so until now, at the time of writing, the summer of 2015. I now do pretty much everything I want and feel healthy and strong. People are always remarking on how well I look and how spectacularly I have healed myself. When I look back five years to 2010, it has been a long road, but such a rewarding one, and the changes both inside and out are profound and life-changing.

Since my ankles healed back in 2013 after we moved away from my mother, my focus has really been on the subtler side of healing and emotional balancing. I sometimes spent hours a day addressing this, and gradually the myriad unnoticed knots of stress so deeply rooted in all of us started to unwind. This aspect revealed itself to me as the true cause of autoimmunity – the body eventually following the mind into imbalance. I have

touched on that in this part of the book, but mainly on my failures in that area. I will be looking at this same journey from a totally different perspective in the third part of this book and will cover all of that in detail, but first let's move on to part two of the book and all the things I did on a physical level to "tame the beast" until the deeper issues could be addressed.

PART TWO
Taming the Beast

⭢ CHAPTER 7
SO WHAT DO I DO EXACTLY?

I'm so glad to be moving on to the second part of this book. Usually I'm a prolific writer; the words flow out of me once I get over my initial laziness in the morning (which has me looking desperately for anything else to do apart from writing), and once I type the first word, I find it hard to stop. However, dragging up the memories of the time I was very ill and chasing around doctors in vain for diagnoses and non-existent cures was hard to write. Now though, we can get onto some far more enjoyable and positive stuff – what to actually do about autoimmunity.

I have hinted at many of the things I did to "tame the beast" in the first part of the book, but in this second part I'm going to run through all the things that were useful to a greater or lesser extent. I'm going to confine this second part of the book to the various physical, dietary and environmental issues which can bring the symptoms down enough to have confidence that you are on the right track. The truth is that the root cause of these illnesses is at a deeper level, more in the realms of the emotional and spiritual, but it's very hard to focus on that and believe in such magic when you are in screaming agony and you are full of the propaganda of the conventional doctors and drug companies.

In days gone by and in other cultures that are closer to nature, healers stepped in with advice, herbs etc at a much earlier stage of any imbalance, when the body was whispering its advice. Nowadays, illness is so much part of the culture, and doctors treat disease rather than promote health. This paves the way for the diseases to get a greater hold, as we are not taught to aim for perfect health, but instead to "control and manage" symptoms. It's a ridiculous state of affairs that allows the body to get into an awful state and to start shouting to be heard. We are not taught to listen to the subtler symptoms, but to cover them up when they become unbearable.

This is why so many branches of natural medicine are not so effective as they once were – they were designed for an age with far fewer environmental onslaughts and a much healthier array of seasonal, unprocessed food. Nowadays when we live in a society full of money stresses, EMFs, fast food and total disconnects with the planet, it is hardly surprising that these gentle healing arts are having trouble balancing us again. This then fuels the dogma of the conventional doctors that anything apart from their own ideas are primitive and ineffectual woo-woo.

So what do we have to do to step out of the hamster wheel of modern medicine and actually find our way to a cure? Right then, let's get to the real essence of this section – a clear set of instructions for those who have been recently diagnosed with autoimmunity, or those who have been in the system for a while and are losing faith in the drugs they have been given.

A note to those who are on medication: I didn't stay on the meds for long, only about six weeks, so I am not an expert on how to get off them. From what I have heard from those who have succeeded and from doctors who actually try to heal their patients properly, you can implement all these techniques while still on the meds. Of course, being on the meds is not ideal, but so many have such a fear of coming off them that they don't even try to really heal, believing it's black and white, one way or the other. Just don't worry about the meds for now. As your symptoms die down you will grow in confidence and you will want to come off the meds – the fear will dissipate.

I must put a caveat in here though, and that is to consult with your doctor about coming off them. There are some that need to be tapered off (such as steroids), and probably other considerations too, so don't just stop cold turkey. If you have a closed-minded doctor then try to find another who will work with you and listen to you. There are more and more of that breed who are getting just as disillusioned as we are with the chemical route, so don't lose heart. One day, you need to get off those meds, as they are all pretty poisonous to the system, but to start with just go through the instructions below and see where you are. In their own time the drugs will fall away, and you will discover the magic on the other side... not least of which is the confidence to take your health into your own hands and not be reliant on doctors ever again unless you run into something immediately life threatening. It's so liberating to take the power back!

So here's a great way to approach autoimmunity in a nutshell and to give yourself the confidence to go against conventional advice. It took me a long time to build up confidence in these methods, but in the following steps I hope to give you the distilled version of this whole book and save you the months and sometimes years of wrong turns I made. You should be able to do this much quicker than I did.

1. Fasting.

Yes, fasting... If you are already 100% convinced that diet is key then this stage is not so important, but if you are coming straight from the doctor with a head full of fear, this is the fastest way to show you there are alternatives. Take in nothing but water for three to five days. Does this sound extreme to you? Well, it really isn't. Not eating for that long is no danger to anyone if done correctly and electrolytes are balanced. Longer fasts, say more than ten days, might need expert supervision, but anyone can fast for five days. If you have never tried it you will imagine it's hell, but only the first couple of days are uncomfortable. After that the lightness of body and mind are a real treat. So why is this the most important move? Because when fasting the digestive system clears itself out and the body can begin to reset itself. By the second or third day you will find that inflammation has died down drastically. The importance of this step is to quickly demonstrate to you that the doctors are way off when they say that diet is not important. You will know for sure that they are wrong.

2. Ketogenic Diet.

Get onto a ketogenic, low carb "paleo" diet. Research Natasha Campbell McBride's GAPS diet and Jack Kruse's Epi-paleo diet and put your trust in them. I have tried many other ways round this, and none have had such a dramatic effect on reducing inflammation. Many of the benefits of fasting can be maintained if you get into ketosis. Don't get into an insane cycle of fasting and then eating sugary stuff then fasting again like I did. It confuses the body. Once you have tasted the magic of fasting, get ketogenic. Don't mess around. The magic is in the bone broths and probiotics from fermented veg etc. Heal that gut! All health begins in the gut!

Diet is about as far as a lot of people go, and even then they usually get it wrong. They turn to vegetarianism or veganism or even raw diets and juicing. I know – I made those mistakes. I won't bang on about whether we are vegetarian or not –but no, we aren't. Eventually most people who have autoimmune problems and research for themselves come across the paleo diet. However, not only is it often misunderstood, but your basic paleo diet, huge as the improvement is over a junk food or grain and dairy based diet, just isn't enough to shift an established disease.

While on the subject of grains, even though we all know these days that they strip the gut of its good bacteria, act like sugars in the system and cause inflammation with their glutens etc, these problems might not even be the worst of their evils. These days they are often treated with potassium bromate. Bromine displaces iodine, which causes all sorts of problems including cancer and interferes with hydration.

Giving up grains, sugars, dairy, pulses and nightshades, great improvements that they are, usually isn't enough. What most people miss is that 50 years ago we wouldn't have had to be so strict with diet as we do today now we face so many other problems. Escalating environmental factors demand more radical diet considerations. I missed this crucial gem of wisdom for a long time. These days to have any chance of reversing autoimmunity, you really need to be in nutritional ketosis, at least temporarily, especially in the northern hemisphere where vitamin D from the sun is scarce and we are designed to eat a lot less carbohydrate.

Use paleotrack.com or similar to input your food and make sure your daily intake of calories is about 60-80% from good fats – coconut oil, olive oil, animal fats etc, keep protein to about one gram per pound of lean bodyweight (determined by calculating body fat percentage and subtracting the fat from your total bodyweight) and keep the carbs to less than 40g, preferably nearer to 20g. This will induce ketosis, but is ketosis enough? Probably not, but it will take sugar out of the equation, which solves a lot of problems. In addition to this, you will need to get going on healing the gut with bone broths and probiotic foods such as unpasteurised sauerkraut. Also, and please don't ignore this step – up your intake of oily fish and shellfish. The massive amount of beneficial nutrients in these beasties, along with their ability to rebalance the body's omega 3 levels make them possibly the best food on the planet. In short, seafood fixes the brain, and without fixing the brain, nothing else gets properly fixed. Try to eat the occasional meal of organ meats too – far more beneficial than muscle meats.

3. Acceptance.

This is so important! Perhaps this should be number one. Do not fight the illness – accept it and love it. There is a lot of truth in the old saying, "What you resist persists". You need to totally change your attitude to illness. See it as an opportunity to discover and clear subtle blocks and to get to a level of health and happiness that you never dreamed possible. If you succeed in this, you have a far greater chance. You will find that an interesting factor comes into play here, what I came to call "the power of the next step". What you are no longer worried about because you have moved on to something more important tends to heal rather quickly. It's amazing how many niggling ailments that had worried me for years disappeared when all I was focusing on was the agony of the arthritis. Once I let those little ailments go and forgot about them in the face of a far more serious concern, the body just cleared them up. But how can you move past an agonising issue to another one beyond it so you can let the body heal? How is it possible to let go of such a horror enough so as to allow the body to do its work? See point 7 coming up…

4. Low Dose Naltrexone (LDN).

Find a doctor who will prescribe this for you. It's about the only safe drug out there at the time of writing, and it will turn down the symptoms another notch to help you focus on what's important. I didn't give in to it for three years, but I would advise anyone to at least take it for a year or so. One warning here – it can be very effective, so the temptation is to rest on your laurels and rely on it. Don't! Remember it is still just symptom control – you are not cured yet. Still listen to the whispers of the body and work on all aspects of healing them. LDN will just give you an easier ride and prevent much of the damage to the body that autoimmunity can cause.

5. Remove Environmental Stressors.

This might sound a bit vague, but having got the inflammatory rubbish out of the diet, may people fail by not addressing the environment. Get rid of harmful non-native EMFs as much as you can, follow your heart in your life and career choices etc. Trust me, stress of all types is at the root of illness. Banish as many as you can. Most people don't heal because they leave too many obstacles in the way of the body's natural tendency to heal. Trust the body. Get out of its way. A note on painkillers: Whatever you do, try to avoid non-steroidal anti-inflammatories and proton pump inhibitors. Doctors give these out like sweets these days, but they offer only temporary relief while destroying the gut, thus making your other efforts pretty useless. Find another way around.

Non-native EMF.

The planet creates its own electromagnetic fields, and we are adapted to these, but in recent decades we have really messed up with our fascination with technology. The big problem we have made for ourselves comes from two main sources – mobile phones and WiFi. Our physiologies are constantly bombarded with these EMFs, and they do untold damage. Even if there is anything mentioned in the press about the dangers, it usually focuses on cancers caused by overuse of mobiles – there is little mentioned about its effect on autoimmune conditions, but the disruption to cellular signalling can cause havoc in the body. I won't get technical here, but EMFs are not only possibly the number one cause of the steep rise in many diseases, but unless they are understood and brought under control very soon, they could even contribute to our extinction. It's that serious.

Don't get the latest mobile phone – the higher the "G" rating, the worse it gets. When you are carrying your mobile phone, have it switched off or at least to airplane mode. When talking on the phone, use the speaker and keep it well away from your head. Use it only for texting and emergencies. Check your text messages every so often then switch it off again. Reconsider letting kids have mobile phones. Their brains are in a delicate stage of development, and the risks just aren't worth it. If you have to get them one for emergencies, get them to turn it off unless they are using it for an emergency call. Don't listen to music with earphones, even if switched to airplane mode. It just puts the EMFs deeper into the brain. Get grounding/earthing mats to use when working on the computer and sleep on a grounding/earthing sheet. Although I have no personal experience of them, also look into Magnetico sleep pads. I have heard that they can be even more effective.

One warning about earthing mats and sheets: Recent evidence has come to light that in certain circumstances they can actually make things worse if you use the cable that allows you to plug it into the house's electricity supply's earth. If the electricity in the house is "dirty" enough, this can come back into the mat or sheet, causing more problems than it solves. There is a way around this, and that's to make sure you use the commonly supplied longer cable and copper rod instead of the plug and run it out of a window or whatever so you are earthed directly to the ground outside. Sure, it's more convenient to just plug it into the earth on the mains, but perhaps best avoided.

If you work on a laptop, use it on battery power, don't put it on your lap and wear orange glasses (see section below on artificial light). Walk barefoot outside as often as possible on the grass or concrete. This will dissipate a lot of the stored EMFs. Get rid of WiFi and hardwire your router to your computer with an Ethernet cable. Inconvenient? Yes, but not as inconvenient as the possible health risks. Our domestic electricity can also be a problem. Want to be really sure? Turn your electricity off at the circuit breaker while you sleep. Job done.

Water and Hydration.

As most people know, our bodies are mostly water, so if we are dehydrated, the cells are not going to be working optimally. Some people never even drink water, relying on fizzy drinks, coffee and alcohol, so it's no wonder there are so many imbalances. Fluoride also plays havoc with hydration.

We need to drink water that is as pure as possible, preferably spring water straight from the source, but not many of us have that option. Glass bottled spring water is perhaps the next best, followed by filtered water as long as your area has reasonable tap water to start with. Don't get caught in the trap of thinking distilled water is a good move. I did, and as I mentioned in detail in the first past of this book, it stripped me of zinc, taking away my sense of taste for two months. Yes, it chelates, but it chelates the good stuff too. Stay clear! However, if you live at the top of a high-rise apartment block, watch a lot of television, work on computers, use a mobile and have WiFi, drinking a gallon of the very best water a day might do no good. There are many more factors to consider including all the other ones here that stop the body hydrating properly even when you drink a lot. It's all connected.

Artificial Light.

You might never have considered this, but it's so important. Our bodies need natural light in the day to trigger cortisol production, and they need darkness at night to trigger melatonin production. If that cycle is messed up, our bodies have very little chance of healing from anything. Our sleep is disturbed, we feel listless during the day and things start to go seriously wrong. When we stay up late, way past sunset, under light bulbs, watching TV and playing computer games or surfing the Internet, our bodies are completely confused. Apart from the cortisol/melatonin problem, there is also the problem of artificial light messing around the cholesterol/vitamin A balance in the brain, which makes hydration almost impossible too, and is one of the reasons so many have high cholesterol – it's certainly not down to eating butter and egg yolks!

It's fairly simple actually. The receptors for this cortisol/melatonin cycle are mostly in the eyes. Paleolithic man never had to deal with blue light after sunset; it just didn't exist. They spent all day outside, soaking up natural light from the sun, and at night they had the light of the moon, the stars, and later, campfires, which give out no blue light. We can trick our bodies though. If you wear glasses with orange coloured lenses such as Blublockers after sunset to cut blue light, and maybe get an app called f.lux to dim the computer screen and take out blue light at sunset, this will do a lot to reset melatonin production. In this way, the TV and computer become your "campfires". You will immediately feel a huge improvement in your sleep patterns. Don't go to bed late though – use that melatonin for a restful night's sleep and go to bed when you are sleepy – listen to the body. At least be in bed by 10pm. Bear in mind the skin also reacts to light, so keep the bedroom dark. When you get up, go outside, watch the sun rise – barefoot preferably to earth yourself at the same time. Get that cortisol pumping.

In the early days of my symptoms, when they were confined to my spine only, I used to go night fishing a couple of nights a week. Even though I ate really bad food, drank beer and smoked cigarettes (which I very seldom did when at home) I always returned home pain-free and feeling energised. I wondered for years exactly why that was, thinking it might be because of the fresh air, or just doing what I loved, and it might have been, but nowadays I am convinced it was mostly because of the lack of artificial light, and the fact that I always saw each sunset and sunrise. My circadian rhythms were in balance, and my body started to heal.

I strongly urge you to check out Dr. Jack Kruse's website, books and podcasts for the mind-boggling science of this. Don't get obsessed with diet alone – take light very seriously!

6. Take On Partners.

This is so important. Doctors are generally not partners. If you find one that is, you are lucky, but even then they will probably be too busy to give you much attention. If you can possibly afford it, enlist the help of a good naturopath or functional medicine practitioner. They have seen it all before, and they have seen it heal. It's a huge step in the right direction. At the very least see if you can make friends with somebody with a similar problem to you and support and encourage each other, swapping knowledge and progress.

7. Balance Your Emotions, Heal Your Soul.

Sounds a bit new agey, right? Well, maybe, but here is the most powerful area of all. Once you get the physical symptoms down DO NOT HESITATE to start delving into the negative emotions and stresses that we all carry at a deep level. I ignored this aspect for a long time. Don't just dabble in it either. Give over most of your day to addressing it. Look into EFT (Emotional Freedom Technique) and Byron Katie's "The Work". You can find lots of free YouTube videos on both. Understand it implicitly and work on yourself literally hundreds of times per day. You won't need to do it forever (in fact it will become automatic). The results can be very dramatic, especially when a massive deep-rooted stress falls right over. Do not ignore this step or you will not get to the true essence of healing. It all comes down to the removal of the subtle stresses that conventional doctors tend to ignore, and which is perhaps the main reason for their lack of success in treating chronic disease.

So what is stress? Well, it's all of the above physical stressors for sure, but it's perfectly possible to get all the above right and yet still have problems. Actually, why is it that so many people eat a horrible diet and stay up late watching tons of TV, yet they are still much healthier than we are? I believe that the answer lies in the way they process stress. Some of us get wound up by the slightest thing, hold on to anger and frustrations and worry all the time. This is like a constant attack on the body, and eventually the body starts to attack itself too. There are several things we can do about this...

We can learn to meditate. This is wonderful for relieving stress and taking us to a place of calm. However, many meditators are still beset with stress of all types as soon as they get up from their meditations. In this case, it's very useful to look at various methods of emotional rebalancing. As I said before, my particular favourites are EFT and Byron Katie's "The Work". I have had staggering results in zapping stresses that even 30 years of meditation didn't touch, and the ensuing physical benefits have been spectacular. After a long time of thinking such techniques were a bit beneath me, I am glad I came to my senses and looked into them. They are very, very powerful. Apart from that, just get out in nature more, be grateful for the things you do have instead of moaning about things you don't have and follow your heart and do what you enjoy. Spend quality time with friends and family too – work less, play more.

8. Throw Out Beliefs.

Belief implies doubt. Doubt holds you back. What you need to do is KNOW this is the way to heal, not to believe it is. Research extensively all the areas covered in these steps. Read the writings of the masters in these areas. Join Facebook groups and forums where you can read success stories from ordinary people and chat to them to share ideas and experiences. The more you immerse yourself in their knowledge, the less you have to believe in anything. You will know from hard evidence that it's going to work for YOU.

So, those are the main steps to take from a standing start. There are hundreds of little refinements you can make, and I'm sure you will all find your own little variations on the theme, but these are the main ones to look at. I hope this has given you an overview of what is needed.

Conclusion.

All of the above come down to one thing really – our disconnection with our genetic history. People who still live in tune with the planet are usually very healthy. Some put this down to their hunter-gatherer diets, and this certainly has an effect, but there are so many more ways that we have become disconnected from our natural way of living. Again I must strongly recommend that you look into the work of Dr Jack Kruse for the EMF science, artificial light and his amazing take on a ketogenic seafood based diet. His various series on EMF, light, water, brain/gut connection, leptin resistance and cold thermogenesis are mind-blowing. For healing the gut and restoring gut flora, please research Dr Natasha Campbell McBride. She has done wonders in this field. For emotional balancing and how it relates to specific physical ailments, please look at Louise Hay, Robert Smith, Inna Segal and Byron Katie. More links to inspirational info can be found on the "Resources" page of my website at pureactivity.net.

⊃ CHAPTER 8
DIET IN DETAIL

The biggest puzzle to me is that modern medicine almost completely ignores the role diet plays in health. Doctors have minimal if any training in diet, and then it's of the wrong sort, advocating high fibre whole grains, avoiding saturated fats and cholesterol and other nonsense including the ridiculous "five-a-day" propaganda. They take the Hippocratic oath, which specifies that they should "above all do no harm", which they inadvertently do with their chemical concoctions and then go on to ignore that Hippocrates also said, "Let food be thy medicine and let medicine be thy food."

So, if you are reading this having just been diagnosed, and your doctor has given you the old line about diet not having any bearing on autoimmunity, or if you have just been sent to a dietician and they have told you to eat lots of bread and pasta and avoid fats and red meat, just sit back for a moment and look at it logically. We have always eaten meats and fats, and we didn't always have these diseases, so it can't be them causing the epidemics of autoimmunity and obesity. We need to look at all the stuff that has been invented recently, around the time we got really sick and obese, and the answer is obviously processed foods, sugars etc. If I walk around a supermarket, I watch as people fill their trolleys with 90% rubbish, stuff I wouldn't even consider to be food anymore. In the light of this, it's not surprising that there's an epidemic of Neolithic diseases; in fact it's a miracle that our bodies last as long as they do before breaking down.

I'm not going to dazzle you with science here; I just want to present you with the things that worked for me and why they worked, and a few things that didn't...

Vegetarianism and veganism.

I am convinced that most benefits derived from veggie diets (presuming they are not based on grains and dairy as so many are) are due to reducing the intake of processed foods rather than it being a healthy way to eat as such. Perhaps there was a time when such diets could cure on their own, as so much has been documented about that, but the nature of the planet now with so much chemical, electrical and artificial light pollution makes them less effective. It's all about the total stress load nowadays from all angles, and we need to be stricter than in past decades. A ketogenic diet does seem to have the edge when it comes to reducing the inflammation of autoimmunity. Time and again I have seen people miserable on the even more severe vegan diets, and when they went on to eat a Paleo template, the improvement in their health and wellbeing was stunning. So, I'm going to say no more about it here. I tried it and it had some temporary benefits, but in the long run it was unsustainable for me and many people who I have consulted with.

The blood type diet.

Made popular by Dr. Peter D'Adamo, who theorised that people with different blood types thrive on different diets. I was convinced by this for a while early in my healing process, and at least it helped to get me off vegetarianism, because according to this way of eating, as an O-type, I am a caveman and should eat all the red meat. However, I am not convinced. Animals, including monkeys and apes, have varying blood types, and they don't eat different diets; they eat what the planet provides. The Inuit also have different blood types, and it would be very inconvenient if one of them didn't get on well with a carnivorous diet.

I have also done experiments of my own, posting threads on Paleo Facebook groups to find out if people who had cured or significantly improved chronic illness with a Paleo template were all O-types. The results were eye opening. I actually had more response from A-types saying how much better they felt and listing the improvements to their health. So, my advice? Listen to the planet, not to the advice of random theorists here and there.

This brings me on to the Paleo diet itself. So, what is it? I think there is a lot of nonsense talked about what is Paleo and what isn't so let's look deeper...

What is the Paleo diet exactly? No really, what is it?

Paleo is such a buzzword at the moment, and as you trawl the Internet it seems that there are a whole load of conflicting ideas about what it actually is. In conversation, people have often say, "Oh yes, that caveman diet – lots of red meat!" or even, "Oh, it's just glorified Atkins isn't it?" and then, more often than not, whether online or in person, a discussion ensues about what Paleolithic people actually ate; whether there were more carbs than protein, or whether they ate honey, or whether they just grubbed around for roots and berries.

Well, I was also caught up in that way of thinking for ages, blatantly ignoring the obvious. Paleolithic man didn't have much of a choice about what he ate, because the planet just provided it, and what the planet provided depended upon the latitude and the season. If he was in Africa, he'd have had a very different diet than if he was in the northern hemisphere.

We have become so used to the word "diet" that to most it generally means some sort of rigid eating plan. You must eat this, and you mustn't eat that... But generally such ideas are memes – irrelevant constructs based on some sort of man-made theories and trotted out by various diet gurus according to their individual conditioning. And this way of thinking is even infiltrating the usually more progressive Paleo community... "You mustn't eat carbs..." "Sweet potatoes are the only "safe" starch..." "Eat tons of coconut oil..." etc.

Well, some of this sort of advice can be rather useful, particularly if you have an inflammatory or autoimmune condition. In this case, usually the gut bacteria is simplified and the gut wall is damaged, and avoiding inflammatory foods such as wheat, omega 6 fats, nightshades and dairy can go a long way to resetting the immune system. But does this make it Paleo? Not necessarily.

If we really want to jump on the Paleo bandwagon we need to look way beyond diet itself, and even then we can only really make educated guesses. If we are to assume that certain evidence is correct and that we did evolve as hunter-gatherers in a time when we were healthier, then we need to look at what the lifestyle of a hunter-gatherer might have entailed. Again, we are making educated guesses based on bone records, common sense and extrapolating on the studies of modern day hunter-gatherer people. Mark Sisson and others have written very knowledgeably about this, so with a hefty nod to them here's how I'd distil the essence of Paleo...

For a start, diet... Well, the world has changed enormously since we roamed the plains or the coastlines, rudimentary weapon or fish hook in hand, so we really can't expect to eat what our ancestors ate. The soil was different; the minerals and vitamins were more plentiful in the (pesticide and fertiliser-free) food, which was teeming with beneficial bacteria. However, we can do our best. We can ask ourselves what the planet would provide, at out locality, and at this time of year. Common sense really – eat seasonal, locally produced, organic food. And for the vegetarians out there – Paleolithic man had probably not invented restrictive religious/spiritual dogma that forbade meat eating, so he was unlikely to feel much sympathy for the animal he was about to spear. Mrs. Caveman would also not be very pleased if he came home empty handed because he took pity on some cute little wild boar at the last moment. No, we've always eaten meat. We'd have starved without it in a lot of places. So, diet is fairly simple – eat what nature gives you. Great as coconut oil is as both a food and a medicine, and I eat a ton of it, if you lived in England like I do, you'd never have found it... or bananas... or mangoes. So, I don't reckon those foods are even Paleo for anyone in the northern hemisphere, but they are if you live in Hawaii.

Then there are the enormous amount of non-diet related disconnects we have these days. We don't feel the seasons on our bodies – we spend the whole time inside to avoid the winter and flood our systems with artificial light. We wear shoes so we are disconnected from the planet's electrons and the planet is disconnected from ours. We use vehicles to get about so we don't have to use our poor under-muscled legs. We starve ourselves of community spirit by spending hours a day chatting on Facebook and other social media to people all over the world who we might never meet, but we don't even know our neighbours' names.

As you can see, we are very far removed from Paleolithic man, and every decade that goes by we are getting even further from him. It's no wonder that our bodies are in a massive crisis and the wave of cancer and other diseases becomes more and more like a tsunami, opening up opportunities for Big Pharma to fill us full of chemicals, which certainly weren't part of Paleolithic man's diet.

But there is one thing above all that I think separates us from nature and how we used to be, and the clue is in the animal kingdom. It's our inability to live in the present, which I believe is the major cause of stress, and stress is the major cause of disease and unhappiness. I might be wrong, but I very much doubt if a cheetah or an antelope are particularly concerned about their pensions, or if they worry that they will be able to pay for their kids to go through college, or if they feel guilt at lying around in the sun in the long, carefree interludes between their life and death confrontations with each other.

We will never go back to Paleolithic times, barring a holocaust of some sort; we are stuck with the modern world and all its stressors, so we have to adapt. One of my favourite sayings is applicable here, "Life is not about waiting for the storm to pass; it's about learning to dance in the rain." However, I'd substitute "health" for "life" for the purposes of this article.

So, my conclusion? The "Paleo diet" is generally nothing to do with Paleolithic times, and generally I reckon it's a complete misnomer. However, if we learn to be present, to pay attention to the perfection of every moment we live without always wishing ourselves into tomorrow or hankering after yesterday, we might just take a step closer to the health that our Paleolithic ancestors (allegedly) enjoyed. We will never get rid of bills, traffic jams and other "troubles", but we can certainly change our attitude towards them and be kind to ourselves instead of always giving in to a tide of stress. Very seldom does anything turn out as badly as we fear it might, so don't waste your health worrying about what probably won't happen. Chill out, enjoy the present and become an urban caveman.

Now, I understand that there might still be some questions about meat eating. So many of us have some aversion to it whether out of concerns about cruelty to animals or some religious or spiritual dogma. Let me see if I can address some of your concerns because I feel it's going to be a hard road if you can take in no animal protein or fats at all.

Should we eat meat? It's not so simple. Here are several things you might not have considered…

So, the debate rages on. Are we vegetarian? Are we carnivores? Are we omnivores? There are so many grey areas and subtleties we need to look at before we can make such a decision. When I was vegetarian I really thought it was just a question of whether to eat meat or not to eat meat. I thought at best we didn't need it, that it was healthier not to eat it and that not eating it was also good for our spiritual development and the planet. This is an area where a lot of vegetarians get stuck.

Let's consider several factors:

Genetics.

There has never been a totally vegetarian culture in human history. Ok, there have been some subcultures, usually religious or spiritual, which have adopted vegetarianism, but the truth is that for millions of years we lived a hunter-gatherer lifestyle, and we ate meat. Bone records can clearly show the percentages of protein, fats and carbs that we ate, so there's no real argument there, and we were healthy. Bone records also reveal the time when the modern ailments started to appear – for example it's clear that the Egyptians started to develop arthritis when they began to rely on grains. Many other problems started to show up too about 12,000 years ago as we settled and began farming.

What many people who argue about what percentage of meat we had in our diets seem to miss is that environmental factors dictate this, so it's different depending on the climate and latitude. From the Masai at the Equator to the Inuit in the Arctic, there has always been meat in the diet. At the Equator there is more sunlight, giving more vitamin D to digest carbs, so there are bananas, mangoes etc. In the Arctic there is hardly any fruit or veg and practically none at certain times of the year. The Inuit ate perhaps 80% or more of their calories as animal fats and the rest were from protein, and they were lean and healthy with few of the modern diseases (until they adopted a western diet, so this wasn't down to magic genetics). Interestingly they never suffered from scurvy either despite their lack of vitamin C intake whereas the Arctic explorers often did. Why? The explorers packed dried rice and beans, a combination of empty calories and intestinal irritants, instead of eating what the location provided. There is also a lot of evidence that we got our bigger brains from meat, or more specifically fish eating. It's very likely that we took advantage of the rich pickings along coastlines as we made our way out of Africa. So, genetically we are adapted to meat.

Meat quality.

I don't consider McDonald's, KFC or other types of processed meat to be real meat. It's made from farmed animals and battery chickens full of hormones, antibiotics and trans fats. If this is what the studies on the dangers of meat eating were done, it's no wonder it got a bad rap. Hunter-gatherers very often leave muscle meat on the carcass except in times of scarcity, taking only the internal organs of the animal – heart, kidneys, liver etc. There is actually far more nutrition in those parts of the animal than, for example, your expensive fillet steak. Harmless and delicious as an expensive grass fed piece of steak is, it's still very far from the most nutritious part of the animal, which displays another way we've got things backwards. When I finally realised that meat was okay, I went mad, eating a whole chicken a day and gorging on sausages and sugar-filled low quality bacon. Unsurprisingly, it hurt. I almost never eat chicken these days, as it has very little nutrition compared to red meat, fish and organ meats, is usually grain-fed even if free range, which is always a problem, especially if you have autoimmunity, and anyway, too much protein is not a great thing either, which brings me to...

How much protein do we need?

The short answer is less than bodybuilders think and more than vegans think. If we eat huge amounts of chicken breasts and egg whites every day, packing in 300 grams and upwards of protein, most of it is just excreted. Actually, that much protein also breaks down as glucose, becoming an honourary carb, thus rendering a low carb diet fairly ineffective and promoting systemic inflammation. Too much of anything hurts. Brushing your teeth is good, but do it all day and your gums will bleed. The truth is we do need protein and the amino acids (and probably other nutrients we have yet to discover) in good animal products, as they are definitely a more complete and digestible source than vegetable proteins, but one gram per pound of (lean) bodyweight is quite enough per day, even for muscle building. The actual requirement might even be less than that. There are so many subtler nutrients in all of our foods that we don't fully understand, so focusing on protein alone is probably a very small part of the picture. The truth is, we just don't know everything, much as we like to think we do. Nature has been working on this stuff for millennia and we've only been studying it for a few decades, so let's not get too cocky and start reducing everything to numbers. Just chew good meat, slowly and consciously, until your body tells you that it's had enough, and that's probably just what it needs.

But meat causes bowel cancer and damages the kidneys, doesn't it?

Erm, no. Even modern medicine is finally catching up. There is no evidence that grass fed healthy meat and wild caught fish do anything but good. I'm sure that the aforementioned processed meats and their additives do a lot of damage, but that's not the good meat we're talking about here. People go on about the pounds of impacted meat found in the bowels of obese Americans, and I'm sure it's true. Firstly, if they ate the diet that humans were supposed to eat, they would not have the leptin and insulin issues that lead to obesity, so I doubt if any of that impacted meat is of very good quality.

Secondly, those oversized guts have probably been horribly damaged by decades of grain and sugar abuse, simplifying the gut flora, distending the shape of the intestines and causing spasticity in the muscles responsible for peristalsis until the meat finds places to hide and fester. This is like one of those bad B movies when an innocent party comes across a body and picks up the murder weapon just as the police arrive. It wasn't the meat in the first place – it was probably the grains and sugars that ruined the gut's ability to digest and excrete the meat. The same goes for the kidneys. There is a lot of nonsense talked about protein being bad for the kidneys. This is like saying walking is bad for your legs. Healthy kidneys are designed to deal with protein and healthy legs are designed for walking. If either is damaged, you run into problems, but neither the protein nor the walking causes the problems.

Is vegetarianism kinder to animals and better for the planet?

Hmm... Good sentiment, but a bit misguided. This is a very complicated subject, which on the surface looks like the vegetarians' trump card. I certainly believed it for many years. However, when you start to look a little deeper, you see that countless species have been made extinct through the vast tracts of land used for planting grains and soya, which has destroyed their habitat. "Ah yes," vegetarians will say, "but most of that is for farmed animals." I'm not sure of the percentage, but certainly a lot of it goes to farmed animals, which is just as bad, as those cows are not designed to eat grains and soya any more than we are. They get sick, are pumped with chemicals to keep them alive and then fed to us in low quality meat products having lived a horrendous overcrowded life on concrete indoors, standing in their own faeces. This is not a vegetarian issue – anybody who cares would be appalled at this. Why not leave the land for grazing and eat the resulting healthy, happy animals? I'll leave it at that, but if you want to look further, check out Lierre Keith, a former proponent of veganism, in her YouTube video "The Vegetarian Myth". She makes some good points.

Lean meat is the best, isn't it?

Again, no. Organ meat is the best (after small oily fish/shellfish), followed by connective tissue and marrow etc, followed by the fattier cuts of meat. In the absence of the western addiction to grains and sugars, animal fats do absolutely no harm and never have. Don't cut the fat off that lamb chop, and stop buying lean bacon. You know the streaky stuff tastes better! (Just get some free-range bacon with no sugars added). Fats are very healing for the gut, help with the absorption of many vitamins and minerals and nourish us down to the mitochondrial level, so don't be afraid of them.

Doesn't eating meat affect your subtler energies?

Living as I do in an area where there are a lot of vegetarian meditators, I come across this a lot, and it's a hard one to argue with because there has been so much backing for the vegetarian lifestyle from many gurus and spiritual leaders down the ages. It is said to interfere with the ability to "transcend", thus making meditation less effective and making the body "rajasic" or "tamasic" instead of the preferable "sattvic", to use the Ayurvedic terminology. I too believed this for a long time. Since then I have given it a lot of thought.

Arrogant as it may seem to go against the gurus, I have to say that when I started to run on fats instead of carbs, not only did my systemic inflammation plummet and my ailments reverse, but my emotions got smoother, and my meditations were deeper and clearer than ever, probably because I wasn't fighting the sugar rush. I found good clean meat in moderation to be no obstacle at all. We can also look at the amount of Indian saints who have died of various nasty diseases including cancer. Some of these guys lived in pollution and EMF free areas of countryside or in the mountains, and were, we presume, free of any emotional or stress-related ailments, so surely that points to their diets? The Hindu tradition is where a lot of this comes from, as it does enjoy its rice and pulse based meals, and I feel that's where the problem lies. Also, to suggest that higher states of consciousness are not possible while eating meat completely dismisses many cultures who have eaten meat and fish regularly and have a long tradition of enlightened masters – the Japanese, the Tibetans, the Australian Aborigines and many more.

Amazingly, if you read Ramana Maharshi's guidelines on whether to be vegetarian or not you find some paradoxes. Ramana is held in tremendously high esteem by millions as one of the greatest sages who ever lived, and has been a massive inspiration to me, but he said himself that even though he recommended vegetarianism, self realisation was perfectly possible without giving up meat, and after self realisation it didn't matter a damn what you ate. He also said that meat actually gives you a stronger body. He was vegetarian; he died of cancer when only 70 years old, and later films of him show definite spinal problems. Nobody's perfect, or they wouldn't be in a human body, and Hindus are not the best dietitians. After all, India is the world leader for autoimmune disease.

There really is nothing wrong with humanely killed grass fed meat and wild fish. Cutting them out of the diet completely can lead to all manner of deficiencies that don't show up until much later, so we fail to see long-term vegetarianism as the cause when such problems do arise. Perhaps the worst thing about cutting meat and animal fats from the diet is not so much their absence, but the fact that they are usually replaced by tons of empty carbohydrates and sugars, and that's where the real problems start. So does this mean you should eat as much meat as you can gorge on without bursting? No. Actually, if you never ate another steak or tuna salad you'd be fine, but if you had three servings of shellfish or small oily fish per week, one serving of liver per week and a couple of egg yolks a day (no, there was never anything wrong with them either) along with the obvious good fats, leafy greens and non-starchy vegetables of as many colours as you can find, you will be far better off than you would be without them.

I agree with Dr Loren Cordain, a professor in the Department of Health and Exercise Science at Colorado State University and pioneer of the Paleo movement – if you choose not to eat meat for religious, spiritual, cultural or moral reasons, then go ahead;

it's your choice, but if you're doing it for health reasons, then perhaps you should reconsider.

It's all about healing the gut! Ketosis and GAPS.

It is becoming increasingly understood that the majority of our immune system resides in the gut. The delicate balance of our immune systems depend upon the balance of our gut flora, and bearing in mind the human body is made up of more bacterial cells than human cells, retaining this balance is paramount for health. It's pretty simple really – sugars and grain-based carbs feed the bad bacteria in the gut, which end up taking over by outnumbering the good guys, and all hell breaks loose in the body. At this point we develop digestive problems, and if they are not addressed correctly, the wildfire of inflammation gets deeper into the body, triggering all sorts of issues, depending upon our genetic predisposition. This can manifest as the many autoimmune conditions from arthritis through multiple sclerosis to the myriad of thyroid problems headed up by the increasingly common Hashimoto's. A damaged gut flora along with the resulting leptin and insulin resistance is also at the root of the huge upsurge in obesity and diabetes. Research is even now showing that starving the body of sugars and getting into ketosis is a very effective treatment for cancer too.

In short, a ketogenic diet is one that swaps the body's primary fuel from glucose to ketones. This is done by reducing the daily carb intake to less than 40g or even down to 20 or so. After 30 days or thereabouts, the body adapts to its new fuel and starts to burn body fat much more efficiently. This is because there is no glucose available so it has to find an alternative source of energy. The result of this is a leaner body without going hungry, a dramatic reduction in systemic inflammation and a regained sensitivity to the hormones leptin and insulin. It's all good! The only downside is that sometimes you can get some discomfort during the initial adaption phase, both from the body learning to burn fat and from the release of toxins contained in that fat. This can usually be offset by keeping well hydrated and balancing the electrolytes by taking Epsom salt baths and putting a little Himalayan salt in your first drinking water of the day.

A wonderful benefit of being in ketosis is that when you run on fats rather than carbs you can go a lot longer between meals, so you are not tempted to grab junk food while out and about. Fats are like putting a nice slow-burning log on a fire, whereas carbs are like newspaper; it burns and it's gone, and very soon you need more. Switch over to the better fuel. You won't regret it!

For further information on the science of ketogenic diets, please look at the work of Phinney and Volek. They have written books on ketogenic living for the general public and athletes alike. Do not be fooled by doctors who say it is some sort of extreme diet that should not be attempted without supervision. If done correctly, it is totally safe.

A lot of our brain and nervous system also resides in the gut, running alongside it in the form of GALT (gut associated lymphoid tissue). Because of this it is hardly surprising that many of the so-called mental and emotional problems also stem from an imbalance in the gut flora. Once you see the pattern, it is easy to understand that the progression of mental disturbances, from hyperactivity and ADD through to Asperger's and autism, are closely linked with gut health. Even depression, bipolar and schizophrenia respond dramatically to a low carb, ketogenic diet. It's criminal really that the medical profession has not put more faith in this simple approach to reversing the many diseases that continue to puzzle them.

The key to healing the gut is the magic of bone broths and fermented foods. Coconut oil is also very soothing for the gut. Extremely nutritious parts of the animal that we badly undervalue in the west are the bones, bone marrow, connective tissues, cartilage etc. In almost all cultures and ancient medical systems, including Ayurveda, there is some sort of reference to the healing power of bone broths. These days we know why. Boiling bones for extended periods of time (I do mine in a slow cooker for about three days) brings out so many minerals and other nutrients that heal the gut, which in combination with fermented foods such as raw sauerkraut can in time seal leaky gut so well that all sorts of seemingly unrelated illnesses vanish. For the full ins and outs of exactly what bone broths can do for you and to research further, look at the work of Dr Natasha Campbell McBride. She is a pioneer in this field and her GAPS (Gut and Psychology Syndrome) diet is basically a very low carb ketogenic diet based around bone broths and fermented foods to seal the gut. She had initial success curing her own son of autism, and has gone on to help millions around the world with both psychological and physiological conditions.

Please research all you can about the GAPS diet. There is lots of information on the Internet about how to implement it and go through the stages of reintroducing foods after some time on the initial phase of just bone broths, probiotics and well-cooked veg. Believe me, it's the way to go.

One thing however, that McBride does not stress enough is the importance of fish. It is here that Jack Kruse excels, so look at his website for that. Simply put, just eat as much shellfish and small oily fish as you can. The DHA, omega 3s and many other anti-inflammatory compounds do more than any other food on the planet to protect and heal. This is doubly important if you have any neurological issue such as MS because the brain and nervous system can never truly heal without a lot of fish in the diet.

WHAT TO EAT AND WHAT NOT TO EAT FOR CALMING AUTOIMMUNITY.

Foods to eat at any time, even in the early stages:

Bone broths.

Fermented veg such as raw sauerkraut.

Well-cooked meat and fish, preferably shellfish, small oily fish, organ meats and beef.

Good fats such as animal fats, coconut oil and olive oil.

Non-starchy veg, well cooked – leafy greens, broccoli etc.

Seaweeds.

Himalayan salt and herbs.

Spices such as turmeric, ginger, cardamom, cumin, coriander, white and black pepper. Avoid the hot ones that are derived from chillies, peppers etc.

Drink only water, or maybe green tea and herbal teas. Don't drink with meals – drink in between.

Foods to reintroduce one at a time when symptom-free:

Eggs, starting with yolks.

Avocados.

Salads if you like them, but they are not really necessary.

Berries. These are the best and least sugary fruits.

Ghee and then good quality grass-fed butter.

High fat cheeses and heavy cream (some may never be able to tolerate any dairy apart from ghee and butter, and a very few may never even tolerate those).

Root vegetables such as carrots, parsnips and sweet potato. Some like to stay in ketosis, in which case limit these or cut them completely.

Mushrooms.

Good nuts such as macadamias, almonds, Brazils and pecans in moderation.

Dark chocolate – 85% or higher, preferably with no soya. This contains resveratrol, which has many benefits including, allegedly, helping to repair some of the damage done by excessive carbs.

Fruits – try to eat in moderation and in season. If you are eating veg you don't really need fruit though, and apart from a handful of berries now and again, they will probably take you out of ketosis.

Foods to just forget about forever. AVOID!!

Grains of any sort. This includes grains that supposedly don't contain gluten, which is probably not even the worst thing in wheat. Just lose the grains completely and anything that's made with them, even if it contains only a trace amount. Just one bite a month can set you back.

Nightshade vegetables – white (Irish) potatoes, aubergine (eggplant/zucchini), tomatoes, peppers, chillies, tobacco. Although some nightshades are good food to those who have no autoimmunity (they will probably not break the gut on their own), once the gut is broken they can be even more painful and inflammatory than grains.

Pulses – lentils, soya beans, kidney beans, chickpeas, peanuts, cashews. They contain lectins, which are very inflammatory.

Manmade oils such as vegetable oils and trans fats. Forget all about "healthy low fat spreads" – they aren't healthy. In fact forget anything labeled "low fat". They have probably replaced the fats with sugars.

Milk and other low fat dairy. It's just the carbs from the cow. Stick to high fat dairy if you can tolerate it. Milk is generally pasteurised anyway, which destroys the lactase that helps to digest the lactose, making lactose intolerance pretty much a given.

"Healthy" seeds like chia, quinoa etc. They really aren't that healthy, and we don't need them. I dabbled when I was ill, and they hurt as much as wheat.

It goes without saying, but all processed foods. If it has an ingredient list on the packet, it's no good.

Sweets, cakes, and artificial sweeteners. This includes the so-called healthy ones like stevia and xylitol. They will not do much harm in themselves, but they do tend to keep our addiction to the sweet taste burning, which can open us up for greater fails. Just lose the sweet tooth if you can – much safer. Don't get caught up in trying all the paleo cheat recipes imitating cakes and bread that are so popular these days. Get used to real food.

Grain-based alcoholic drinks such as beer and whisky. If you find you can reintroduce alcohol at some point, stick with red wine in moderation and clear spirits such as tequila, vodka and gin. Use soda water for mixers and maybe a squeeze of lime or something non-sugary.

My own diet journey.

For a long time I was very strict with my diet. I went pretty much with the GAPS programme, but making sure I ate a lot of fish too. There was a time when I could only eat well-cooked meat, fish and veg. I could not even take ghee or butter, so I gave up dairy completely. I stopped all fruit too, as I could feel the discomfort from the sugars. For some reason, dark chocolate never bothered me, except for the caffeine content when my heart was misfiring, which made it worse, for obvious reasons. For me it was the starch in anything that caused the most inflammation.

I have since reintroduced berries and the occasional apple, and I am so glad that I can also take dairy to the extent that I can have butter and a little cheese. I did go mad on cream for a bit, but I limit it, as although it doesn't hurt my joints any more, it does give a little heartburn sometimes, particularly when combined with eggs, so my body clearly isn't 100% happy with it.

The main advantage about being so strict for so long is that most of the desire for bad foods has disappeared. I no longer run around trying to find alternatives to bread or trying to make vegetables look like rice or pasta. I now actually love simple food – meat, fish, eggs, fats and veg, and 99% of my diet is made up of these. I am happy with fewer ingredients, flavoured in various ways with herbs and spices. It is also so simple when shopping too – you hardly ever need a list and can keep to just one or two aisles in the supermarket, or preferably your local butcher, greengrocer or farmer's market.

Here is a massively important point: When you eat is often more important than what you eat. There is so much discussion about when to eat or how many meals per day to eat, but it's much simpler than that! Refine your tastes until you crave the natural foods and your addictions have disappeared, and just eat what you fancy (from the list of real foods) when you are hungry, stop when you are full, and repeat! I have no set mealtimes. I might eat once per day, or I might eat twice, but never more than that, and no snacking. I wait until I'm hungry and then eat. This is seldom early in the morning, which is the time the body is naturally detoxing, so I tend to just drink a lot of water before midday and then eat a large meal at about 2pm, or maybe two smaller ones at about 10 or 11am and 4 or 5pm. I never eat close to bedtime either, as that always triggers digestive problems and inflammation, even if it's good food.

All of this might seem very strange to start with, but once the body gets used to these real foods, it is not only healing, but totally satisfying. No dieting, no calorie control, no going hungry... The feeling of knowing every mouthful you take is feeding health is much better than the Russian roulette of the regular westerner's diet. After a while you can pretty much say goodbye to doubts, and even to fears of future illness.

Right, I think that's got diet pretty much covered. Let's go on to the other, non-diet related factors that will help to tame the beast of inflammation.

⊃ CHAPTER 9
OTHER AREAS TO LOOK AT

In the beginning when inflammation is raging, it can be hard work to keep on top of it, but that stage soon dies down... Trust me, it's not forever. What I'm going to look at in this chapter are the methods I found really useful for calming symptoms. Apart from the emotional balancing techniques, I don't think that any of the methods in part two of this book are actually cures for full-blown autoimmunity at the deepest level, but they will take the symptoms down to a level where you are not so swamped with the horror of the pain, so you can start to look deeper. Having significant success with the more physical methods listed here can give you some great confidence that you're on the right track anyway.

Having said that, you might well find that you do cure some of the minor niggles and ailments, particularly as I've mentioned before, if you are not focusing on them too much. The body has a habit of healing things when you've forgotten about them; one day you wake up and remember that used to have such and such a problem but you can't quite pinpoint the moment, perhaps months previously that it vanished.

Most people, as long as they have avoided or given up the conventional methods, will initially be looking at the more concrete physical methods such as diet and herbs and do not look deeper, but there are some who go the other way and discount anything short of the subtler things like emotional balancing, meditation, healing etc. However, this can be a little premature. This can be the case with the more spiritual type people who get ill and then decide it's all down to kundalini shifts, alien intervention or sunspot activity when it's quite simply that they have been eating rubbish for decades. To illustrate, there is absolutely no point in polishing a muddy car.

Hose the mud off first and then see if there are any scratches and dents that need to be filled in and painted before you even think of polishing it. The previous chapter about diet was about hosing the mud off, whereas this chapter is all about the dents and scratches (and a little polishing with the EFT etc), but for the full polish, you'll have to wait until part three.

I have already covered some things that did work in previous chapters, especially in chapter 7 and chapter 8, but below are a few of the things I haven't touched on.

It's also worth mentioning the many things I did try that didn't work or only had a minimal effect, even only to stress that the beneficial things I do list are by no means the only things I tried. I went through hundreds of techniques, quick fixes and potions that were utterly useless. I'm sure you will try lots of things yourselves and experiment, and I'd encourage that, as you might well find something that I overlooked, and if so, please let me know.

So among many others, what I consider to be of minimal use and not worth focusing on, particularly if you have limited time are: Hulda Clarke zapper/parasite cleanse (unless you have some evidence that you have parasites, in which case I'm still suspicious), drinking peroxide solution, most vitamins and herbs, including Ayurvedic (maybe useful in the "polishing" stage but not much use when in agony), Swedish bitters, castor oil packing, Bentonite clay (to clean intestines), alkalising diets (the body takes care of its own pH balance despite what you eat), copper bracelets and heel pads, apple cider vinegar (except for malic acid during a liver flush), juice fasting (expensive and often sugary), topical ointments and oils of all types (look deeper than rubbing stuff on joints).

I do admit that some of the above have some uses, but they do not have the dramatic effect that subtracting the major stressors can have. Try to get out of the pills and potions mentality.

EMFs, Artificial Light and Earthing

I'm not going to go into detail about this again, as I've covered it in chapter 7, but in case anybody is browsing this chapter first or missed it, please look back at that because it is as important, if not more so, than diet. You will not heal properly no matter how good your diet is if you do not take away or minimise these dreadful stresses.

Liver Flushing

This since it is one of the most dramatic techniques I used, and although I'm still not convinced it actually works as it's supposed to, it definitely does something and brings inflammation down. As I mentioned in chapter 5 in the first part of the book, I did 34 of these flushes, mostly monthly, but sometimes two-weekly. They used to give me a few days of significantly reduced inflammation, but whether this is simply down to a clearing out of the digestive system or actually expelling the build-up of soft intra-hepatic stones as it's supposed to do is still an area of contention. Many say that it's an absolute con, and that there are no soft intra-hepatic stones in anyone's liver. They say that the green globs floating in the toilet the next morning do not originate in the liver but are actually made in the stomach from a process of saponification from the olive oil and other ingredients combining with the bile from the liver. This doesn't ring completely true to me, because it's quite possible to get literally hundreds of stones out in one flush, then only a few or none the next time... and then back to hundreds. If it was purely saponification then surely the results would be more consistent? As it is, the varying amounts of stones expelled does tie in with the theories of one bile duct emptying while another is clogged, which then finally lets the stones go a few flushes later.

To be really honest, I don't know, but I have included liver flushing because for a long time it was the highlight of my month due to the relief it gave me from the agony. I would recommend that you read Andreas Moritz's book "The Amazing Liver and Gallbladder Flush" for the full information about it, but if you want to give it a go, here is a brief description of the technique to get you started:

Drink apple juice, about two litres a day for six days, or to avoid the sugar overload, a few tablespoonfuls of cider vinegar in water three times a day, or malic acid tabs/powder... You're just going for the malic acid (which apples and cider vinegar contain) to soften the stones. During this time, eat a light diet, not too much fat as this primes the liver to store bile so it can fire more out on the main flush day (the only excuse ever for low fat eating!). Then on the day of the flush, don't eat after 2pm. Mix four tablespoonfuls of food grade Epsom salts in a big jar/jug so you can split 800ml into four 200ml glasses. Or just mix a tablespoonful into each 200ml glass – up to you, but it dissolves better if you leave it to soak... Take one glass at 6pm, then one at 8pm. This will open the bile ducts in the liver and gallbladder, so now you have soft stones, and the ducts are open and ready for action... Then mix half a glass of olive oil with half a glass of squeezed grapefruit juice, shake it up and drink it quickly at 10pm, while standing next to your bed. This theoretically triggers the liver and gallbladder to expel the bile, and with it the stones, through the open ducts, having softened them with the malic acid.

After drinking the olive oil, lie down immediately and don't move for 20 minutes, then sleep if you can. You will feel all sorts of things going on, and you might feel quite nauseous in the early hours (or you might be fine). In the morning take another glass of Epsom salts when you wake, but not earlier than 6am, then another glass two hours after that. At any time from the early hours to the morning you will start to have diarrhoea, which will hopefully contain lots of stones, anything from 50 or so to several thousand, of all shapes and sizes. The green ones float, as they are mostly fatty deposits, but the larger and denser tan and black ones (if you have any) will probably sink. Some people poo into a sieve to see them all and count them to know how many they have got rid of, but you can get a pretty good idea without that sort of unpleasantness. Eat lightly that day, starting with a little fruit a couple of hours after the last Epsom dose. Stay close to the toilet!

I must put a caveat here that experts generally say to have professional colonic irrigation or at least an enema two days after the flush to make sure the last of the stones are expelled, as the theory goes there are a lot of toxins in them, which can be a problem if they stay in the gut. I have tried both colonics and enemas, but most times haven't bothered, and have never run into any trouble.

Repeat once a month until you have two flushes clear of stones, and then do three flushes a year or so as maintenance.

Now, I have to point out that many conventional doctors think that this is a dangerous procedure. I can understand their point of view maybe when you apply it to those with serious gallstones and the possibility of getting one stuck in a bile duct triggering a medical emergency, but this can happen anyway, and since many have actually shifted gallstones with this method, I'd say it's actually worth the risk if it could potentially save your gallbladder from being ripped out.

Anyway in all my 34 liver flushes I have never had any ill effects apart from some slight nausea in the early hours two or three times from eating too much or too late on the day of the flush. But still, try it at your own risk!

Improve Your Sleep

Sleep is so very important to healing. The immune system will not reset itself without regular decent nights' sleep.

So many people these days have trouble sleeping. Yet again, it's a matter of finding the disconnects that modern life has brought about and filling the gaps, so here is my guide for how to get a better night's sleep. Please don't ignore the parts that deal with artificial light and EMFs. Because they haven't been talked about before very much when dealing with this subject, and many think it's enough to have a cup of chamomile tea in front of the TV, it's easy to ignore them, but they are perhaps the most important factors.

1. A good night's sleep begins with how you spend your day. Get up early, go outside, look at the sunrise and get your bare feet on the Earth. Get the cortisol going so you're in synch with nature's daily cycle. This will help the melatonin cycle to kick in later on when you need it for sleep.
2. If you drink tea and/or coffee, try to keep them to before 4pm, or preferably midday.
3. Same with alcohol. If you drink, do it in moderation and make sure it's worn off by bedtime. An evening spent boozing never gave anyone restful sleep.
4. Don't eat after 8pm, or preferably 6pm if you have trouble sleeping. Give it at least two hours before bedtime, and don't eat heavily in the evening.
5. If you are overweight, sleep apnea can be a big problem, ruining restful sleep. Cut the carbs and lose that excess blubber.
6. Wear orange glasses, such as Blublockers, after the sun has gone down to cut blue light from the eyes when it's not supposed to be there. The main receptors for melatonin production are in the eyes, so if you are under artificial light or watching TV/computers all evening,

melatonin production will be affected. Orange glasses will lessen the effects of artificial light.

7. Don't watch TV in the evening at all if you can help it, and certainly not programmes that are overstimulating. Want to watch a zombie or vampire movie? Watch it in the morning!
8. Magnesium is huge in aiding restful sleep. Take some magnesium malate at bedtime, spray on some magnesium oil or take an Epsom salt bath.
9. Take a cold shower or bath sometime before bed, maybe after a warm Epsom salt bath, until you get cold adapted and it becomes easier. I won't go into the science of this, but believe me, the combination of orange glasses and the cold is magical for sleep.
10. Yes, chamomile tea is good too! But don't drink too much of any liquid before bedtime or you might need to go to the bathroom too many times. Hydrate earlier in the day.
11. Don't exercise vigorously before bedtime. Exercise in the morning or late afternoon. If you feel the need to do something, gentle yoga or Hanna Somatics are ideal and can really help restful sleep. Too little exercise is bad for sleep, but too much is worse...
12. Don't overdo cardio exercise at any time of the day. It totally disrupts hormonal systems. Get into abbreviated weight training and sprints instead. To lessen the impact of cardio workouts with some very clever Ayurvedic ideas, see my blog posts on it on my website at pureactivity.net or for greater detail, get my Pure Activity book.
13. An Ayurvedic idea this one, for balancing vata dosha, which is the dosha that's out of balance when we can't sleep. Perform an abhyanga, or oil massage. It only takes a few minutes, and you can do it yourself. It really does help. At least oil the scalp and soles of the feet. Sesame oil

is traditionally the best, but olive oil or coconut oil are good substitutes. I know this seems odd to us in the west, but just put a towel on the pillow to stop it getting oily and wash it out of your hair in the morning. The small inconvenience is worth a great night's sleep, and it does work!

14. Another Ayurvedic principle, but based in science and common sense too is to go to bed when the first wave of tiredness comes; certainly be in bed by 10pm. 10pm until 2am is the time when the body repairs itself the most, and sleep taken between these times is very precious.
15. Turn off the radiator to keep the bedroom cool and open a window or two. A hot, stuffy bedroom is no good for restful sleep.
16. Sleep on an earthing sheet. This is amazing for improving sleep. For millions of years we slept on the ground, exchanging ions with the Earth. These days it is even more important to discharge the body's store of EMFs that we get from our technology. Invest in one!
17. Fit blackout blinds in the bedroom. The darker it is, the better. There are also some receptors in the skin, not just in the eyes, so this can help a lot. Failing this, wear a comfortable silk sleep mask over the eyes.
18. Take all electrical appliances out of the bedroom or unplug them. EMFs can totally disrupt sleep. Certainly never have your mobile phone under the pillow. If you have to have it next to the bed to see the time, turn the brightness down, keep it on airplane mode and keep your orange glasses next to the bed and put them on before you look at it. I can't stress this enough – one blast of blue light can totally reset the body to make it think it's daytime and time to wake up.
19. In the same vein, if you go to the bathroom in the middle of the night, don't turn the light on. If you have to turn a

light on for some reason, put the orange glasses on first.
20. Have sex, with a partner, or with yourself if you have no partner. An orgasm is great for a restful night!
21. If you do wake up, don't fight to go to sleep and try to suppress thoughts. That's impossible and will get you nowhere. Just watch the thoughts come and go without resisting, as if they were a film, and don't attach to them. Stay relaxed and in the present, being thankful for a restful time when you can just lie there and enjoy being you without any pressing responsibilities. If you meditate, this is a good time to do it, but if you don't, just try focusing on your breathing. Just breathe in and out with awareness and this will bring you into the present again. Worrying about not sleeping is the best way not to sleep! Enjoy being awake and before you know it, you'll be asleep again.
22. If you have certain specific worries that are keeping you awake, learn EFT (Emotional Freedom Technique) or look into Byron Katie's "The Work"... or both... This will do wonders for clearing those useless beliefs that keep you stressed. You CAN change your thoughts and beliefs about problems so they don't worry you way before the problems themselves get resolved. It's all about how we look at things, not how things actually are. Stress is a huge killer of people as well as sleep. You will never get rid of all your problems, so get rid of worrying about them instead, and you will never have another problem again!
23. As a very, very last resort you can use supplemental melatonin, but only temporarily, and preferably just to reset the system in emergencies like jet lag. If you do all, or most, of the above, you really shouldn't need it.

Enemas

The first time I did an enema myself, it felt so alien. 200 or so later, they were just a regular part of my daily routine, and I hardly ever lost control of the appliance and sprayed poo all over the bathroom – well, only twice. I just bought an inexpensive home enema kit from eBay and used warm filtered water. I tried other things like coffee enemas, but saw no real extra benefit.

All I can say is try them if you have active inflammation or any digestive issues or constipation. I am not sure why they kill inflammation so quickly, but I suspect it's because it removes a lot of the substances from the gut that are leaking through and the body is reacting to, so it can be almost instant relief. I know most people will not have the time, inclination or patience that I did, but if you do, give it a try. I would recommend consulting with a good naturopath for full instructions.

You can also add dedicated probiotics to the enemas, and I think this is actually a very good way to repopulate the lower digestive tract where oral probiotics might not reach.

Am I absolutely sure they are necessary? No. I did a lot of them at a time when my diet was not as good as it should be, but if you have a really good ketogenic or GAPS diet, I suspect the indignity of enemas is something you might not have to suffer.

Natural Anti-Inflammatories

I know how tempting it can be to take NSAIDs – non-steroidal anti-inflammatories – like Ibuprofen (Advil)) in the early stages, but please resist. If you really need to kill the pain for a bit, and everybody deserves a day off now and again, take Paracetamol (Tylenol). It's just a painkiller, and although far from ideal, it does not wreck the integrity of the gut and destroy the gut flora in the same way as the anti-inflammatory drugs do. Avoid NSAIDs including Cox 2 Inhibitors like Aspirin.

There are some good natural anti-inflammatories though, which could be worth looking into. My favourite was a cocktail of turmeric and boswellia, a herb that can be easily found in capsule form in health food stores or online. I used to put about one or two teaspoonfuls of turmeric in some water and swill down three boswellia capsules as and when I felt I needed them. Ginger is also anti-inflammatory, and although I never took it, I'm hearing some very good reports about astaxanthin, so do look into that.

I also used to drink a lot of concentrated cherry juice and eat pineapple for the bromelain, which are both supposed to have almost magical anti-inflammatory properties, but I think the huge sugar overdose counteracts that.

There are so many herbs and powders etc that are touted as anti-inflammatory, so experiment. You never know...

Sulphur and MSM

Methyl Sulphonyl Methane is an inexpensive white powder available easily online or in health food stores. It is said to help out with joint health by replacing lost sulphur. Now, some new theories that you probably won't hear from your doctor say that the body loses cartilage because of a bad diet that doesn't contain enough sulphur, and of course the grains etc that strip the body of so many good things including sulphur. The body stores a lot of its sulphur in the cartilage, so if it gets low, it starts to use that, and in turn we lose cartilage. Now, the doctors say that it's impossible to replace lost cartilage, and perhaps it is for those who stay on the same diet that got them ill, but if you are willing to make some changes, there's no reason why you can't regrow lost cartilage, at least to a certain extent. A few months replacing the sulphur with daily doses of MSM might just do the trick, as long as you sort your diet out and include lots of sulphur containing foods like egg yolks and leafy greens.

This is definitely something that people with osteoarthritis should consider, but of course cartilage is also lost in joints that have suffered damage from inflammatory arthritis too, so MSM is a good bet all round. After all, the actor James Coburn credited MSM alone with finally curing his severe arthritis.

Vitamin D/K/B12

It is fairly widely known now that vitamin D is very important for health. Even regular GPs test for vitamin D deficiency and prescribe oral supplementation. This is sometimes not such a good idea. Okay, vitamin D helps with the absorption of calcium among other things, but on its own it does not tell the body where to absorb the calcium, so it can end up in the prostate, arteries etc instead of the bones, which is where we want it.

This is where vitamin K comes in. It acts with vitamin D as a kind of traffic policeman telling the calcium to go into the right places like the teeth and the bones. There is no need for calcium supplements. A good diet, even dairy free, can provide easily enough as long as we are absorbing it.

Of course, it's far better to get your vitamin D from sun exposure, so do this as much as you can, lying in the sun at midday with no sunscreen for just long enough to go a little pink (if you have a pale skin), but not to burn. Remember that if the sun casts a shadow of your body that's longer than you are tall, it's too late/early in the day to produce much vitamin D. Remember not to wash straight after either, as this also helps to absorb it.

Many of us live in the northern hemisphere where there isn't much sun even in the summer, so maybe you will need to supplement. Remember to choose vitamin D3 over D2 – much more effective. I'd actually recommend anyone who hasn't already tried it to take vitamin K for three months or so just to strip any existing calcifications from the arteries and anywhere else, because it is very effective at that and certainly can't do any harm as long as you stay within the RDA. There are many good brands out there, but make sure it's vitamin K2, some of which are combined with vitamin D3 if you are deficient.

It is also worthwhile getting tested for vitamin B12 deficiency. If need be this can be replenished by sublingual tablets or injections. Again, it's more a matter of absorption. If the gut flora is balanced and healthy, we should absorb, and indeed perhaps even manufacture, all the B12 we could ever need.

Electrolytes – Magnesium, Sodium and Potassium

Balancing electrolytes can have a huge effect on the health of so many bodily systems. It is said that almost everybody in the western world is deficient in magnesium, and symptoms can range from fatigue and insomnia to heart palpitations and everything in between. Any sort of stress including bad diet can deplete magnesium, and big stresses such as a general anaesthetic can seriously lower your levels. If your electrolytes are out of whack you will not be able to hydrate properly either.

It is very wise to take some time to replenish your magnesium stores. Most of the types of magnesium pills available in health food stores are not very absorbable, but I always had good success with magnesium malate. Magnesium L-Threonate is said to be the better choice if you have any neurological issues such as multiple sclerosis. Remember that you can also get magnesium through the skin, so magnesium oil sprays and Epsom salt baths are also very useful.

When in ketosis from a low carb diet, balancing electrolytes becomes even more important. Remember to also keep your sodium intake up through adding enough salt to your food and daft as it may sound, take a few pinches minimum to a half teaspoon of Himalayan salt in some water first thing in the morning. This little trick can help out with many symptoms. Don't forget potassium too – another important electrolyte. Bananas are a good source, but avocados might be a better choice if you want to avoid sugars.

Also, if you have psoriasis or eczema, which I used to, and which is so common in autoimmunity, Epsom salt baths and soaking affected areas in Dead Sea salt in water can really help with the symptoms until a healed gut gets rid of it altogether, as it did with me.

Chiropractic and Massage

This can be so helpful in arthritis – maybe not at a time when the joints are very inflamed, but when you get on top of the inflammation both chiropractic and massage can be very useful. Chiropractic can shift the tension and subluxations that can feel like arthritis and be blocks to the smooth passage of energy around the body. Massage can really help to break up the knots in the previously inflamed tissues too. Both come highly recommended.

Cannabis Oil

Although I had no experience of this during my own healing, I cannot ignore the amazing evidence that I have heard and read about the healing powers of cannabis, particularly the concentrated oil. It is well documented that it has a track record for wiping out various forms of cancer, even some of the very stubborn brain cancers, but there is increasing evidence that it might also be very useful for autoimmunity. Of course it is still illegal in most places, which seems very odd since it is often touted as the most medicinal plant on the planet.

It seems that it works by acting on the body's own endocannabinoid system, but exactly how is still a mystery. Let's hope that some proper research is eventually done on this wonderful herb so that its properties are more widely accepted and it becomes available to those who really need it.

To find out more, check out Rick Simpson's website, Phoenix Tears.

Exercise

When you are very ill it might not be possible to exercise at all, but when a change of diet has brought the symptoms down, see if you can ease into a gentle exercise routine. All my adult life I have done yoga, but there was a time when I couldn't even manage that, which is when I discovered Hanna Somatics.

Somatics is not so well known as some other forms of gentle exercise, but is widely becoming accepted as perhaps one of the most comprehensive systems to keep the body healthy, supple and pain free. Here's how it works:

Somatic movement education is a system of neuromuscular education that allows more ease and freedom of movement in our bodies. It teaches us to recognise and release chronic patterns of pain, caused by illness, inflammation, repetitive strain, bad posture, injury or stress. These simple, slow exercises are normally performed comfortably on the floor, and can unwind and unlock the holding patterns in the neuromuscular systems that can cause so many deep-rooted physical problems.

The great thing about somatics is that it is totally based on awareness. To be totally aware of all sensations arising during the movements can soon give you a tremendous insight into your own unique imbalances. Developing a deep understanding of your body and its needs instead of relying on others is always the first step to improving health.

Nobody can know your physiology like you can, and with the help of somatic movement you will learn to recognise and release even the most subtle and deep-seated imbalances, which can cause havoc in the body far beyond just aches and pains.

The various categories of movements can be practiced in many ways according to your needs at any given time. The daily cat stretch, a general maintenance routine of half an hour or so is wonderful for regular loosening of any little knots there might be, leaving you feeling rejuvenated for the day.

If however, you have any specific discomfort, such as shoulder pain,or thoracic spine pain etc, you can focus your attention on the specific routines for that area, returning to a more general routine once those imbalances are addressed and comfort returns.

For some it might seem like the exercises are just too gentle, as they did to me when I first discovered them through my good friend, osteopath and somatic movement educator Brian Ingle, N.D., D.O., with whom I have teamed up on my website at pureactivity.net to make these systems more widely available.

I had been involved in yoga for years, normally considered a gentle system, so I should have been more open than most, and yet I still had my doubts. Having practiced somatics for some time now I consider them to be utterly extraordinary, and wish I could find the words to express just how powerful these gentle movements are, and how deeply they affect the physiology.

So many of our ailments can be caused by breaks in the flow of energy in the nervous system caused by tense and locked muscles. Smooth out those kinks and be amazed at how many of your little niggles (or even big ones) might loosen their hold.

Once you are well on the way to recovery you can get back to some walking and other gentle exercise like cycling, or my particular favourite when still healing up – rebounding. I found this so useful when my joints were too delicate to put up with the shocks from hard ground, and rebounding really gets the lymphatic system moving too, which is never a bad thing. I also bought an inversion table. Apart from the obvious benefits of reversing gravity to give the internal organs a rest and a bit of a massage and it being another way to help the lymphatic system, it is wonderful for stretching out and freeing up locked joints. My back always feels so much better after ten minutes on the rebounder and then hanging upside down for a while. In fact I still use this little routine as a warm-up before my weight training sessions.

When the inflammation is under control maybe progress to HIIT (high intensity interval training) and abbreviated weight training. It's very likely that you will have some form of muscle wastage after an illness, particularly arthritis, so building it up again is very important. Healthy functioning of the internal organs depends on a sufficient level of muscle mass too, so it's not just a cosmetic concern. I have covered these in detail on my website and in my previous book, Pure Activity. Just avoid jogging and "chronic cardio". It's a myth that it's actually good for you; it stresses the heart and joints and even shortens your telomeres, perhaps the most accurate marker for health and longevity.

See my book, Pure Activity and my website at pureactivity.net for more info on exercise, and if you like, you can also buy a Hanna Somatics instructional video download there.

Healing

Many things come under this category – Reiki, Quantum Touch, etc. Also there are countless books on how to heal yourself using some sort of energy medicine, chakra balancing etc. My own view is that I didn't get so much out of them unless they put the onus back onto the individual to be responsible for their own healing and to look at deeper levels of themselves. However, I have heard some great reports of miracle cures, so by all means experiment with any that take your fancy. They can do no harm. I guess my path was just destined to be a little more hands-on, and I'm grateful for that. It has stood me in good stead for the future to be confident of healing myself again without having to rely on anybody else.

EFT/The Work

I have mentioned again and again the importance of looking into emotional balancing, and I just have to mention them again here. Look them up, particularly Robert Smith's FasterEFT.com and Byron Katie's TheWork.com. Watch the many free videos out there and get the hang of it.

But there is one thing that is so very important – if you do it halfheartedly you will get few if any results. Devote yourself to it – practice hundreds of times a day on every little issue that comes up, and in time it will become almost an automatic process. The more diligent you are at it, the less time you will have to do it for. It's not something that you will have to consciously do for the rest of your life. After some time you will have a sort of automatic protection against any nasty little niggle that comes up.

A great sage called Papaji was once asked if he had the same thoughts as he had before his awakening, and he said, "Of course, but I just don't believe them anymore."

Aim for that.

A caveat about emotional balancing – don't forget to follow your passion!

Useful, and indeed often miraculous, as emotional balancing techniques can be, there can be a danger of overusing them and lapsing into a state of complacency as you force yourself to love everything that is. Now, it's a wonderful thing to learn acceptance and surrender, but if the situation is very bad, such as an abusive spouse or a house full of harmful mould, there is no shame in getting the hell out of the situation. You don't have to tap and tap until you love being beaten up or having respiratory problems. Just leave. Acceptance is also accepting that the situation you are in is dangerous and you need to do something about it.

Of course there are instances where it isn't quite so clear-cut, and I have one simple test to see whether you should learn to love something or to get it out of your life: Does learning to love it interfere with your passion?

I'll give the example of drumming: I actually got myself to the stage when I was ill that I accepted that I might never play again. By the time I could play again, I also accepted that I might never be in a band. When I was back in a band I accepted that I might never play to my full potential. I was an acceptance junkie. Then one day I sat down and really asked myself what my real passion was. The answer came – to play drums so fluently that there was no gap between my ideas and their execution. I was good on the drums, but certainly no virtuoso. That might be good enough for some, and there have been some wonderful sounding drum tracks played by non-virtuosos, but my heroes on the drums are all virtuosos, and I hear in my head far more than I can actually play.

I decided to really practise to fill all the gaping holes in my technique. I knew my weaknesses and knew exactly what to do about them, and the first day I sat down at my practice kit was one of the most fulfilling for years. Not only did I make quick progress and really enjoyed myself as new abilities opened up to me, but a bit of a miracle happened... My left knee and right wrist, the last two joints on my body with some slight niggles, immediately felt tremendously better and continued to improve in comfort and mobility. Since I am pretty much convinced that knee issues are down to the feeling of not moving forward in life, it is no surprise that this helped the issue massively.

So, never let go of your dreams. Use EFT and other techniques not to just learn to love everything that's bothering you, but also to inspire you to follow your passions. We have passions for a reason – they usually lead us to what our life's path really should be, and if we love what we do, we get a big boost up the ladder to loving all that is, and from that comes true health.

Working with dreaming for healing and beyond.

When we're on a healing journey of any sort, the tendency can be to look outside ourselves for the answers. We run around from doctor to doctor; we sit and trawl the Internet for hours a day and worst of all, we panic and worry. What would serve us far better is to develop our own intuition so we can tune in to what the next step should be directly from the source... from ourselves.

However, when we are worried about some ailment, particularly if it's a recent diagnosis, I can understand that it can be difficult to be settled enough to tap into that source. It is here that dreaming can come to our rescue...

In the early days of my healing journey, even though I always thought of myself as a spiritual person, when faced with agonising joints and therefore high stakes (in the sense that if I didn't recover there could be dire consequences to my mobility), I started to doubt that such magic was possible. Among the lorry load of books I read were some books on the use of dreams in healing.

A very good tip I can give is on remembering your dreams. If you don't remember them, there isn't very much you can learn from them. To remember a dream you need to really focus on it the very second you wake up. Stay in the same position and don't open your eyes until you have run the dream through in your head. Also, keep a pad and paper by the bed, and when you have the dream clear, write it down. Just now, on reading through my dream diary that I kept while I was ill, there were several that I had absolutely zero recollection of even though I had written them down, and some that I got more insights from, even three years later as I write this. It shows the power of writing them down!

One other idea is to help you to "guide" your own dreams in the direction you want them to go. Just falling asleep at night can result in any old random dream, some of which might be useful to you, but some not. To increase your chances of dreaming about the issue that's important to you, just gently think about it as you fall asleep, and maybe even ask quietly to be shown something you need to be shown.

This might seem like a load of mumbo jumbo to some people, but look at it like this: in dreaming, we are still ourselves, but when disconnected from the stresses and tribulations of a sick body, deeper intuition can be accessed, which, upon waking, can be applied to everyday life.

In my own experience, after writing down a few of these dreams, a pattern started to form. The dreams didn't always give a clue as to exactly what to do next, although I certainly got some ideas; more often they gave encouragement and confidence that I was on the right path and that success would eventually be mine, even though I was going against conventional ideas and the advice of doctors.

After a while, once confidence is gained in the messages one gets while in the dreaming state, it's possible to tap into that very intuition while wide awake. Then, the deeper the connection with that intuition grows, the faster we can find answers and notice the wonderful clues that nature gives us along the way, which otherwise might be covered up with panic and fear. This is just one of the amazing ways that illness can be such a blessing.

To take this idea to its ultimate conclusion, dreaming might just be one of the clearest pointers to the ultimate truth of our nature, and one of the few ways that the mind can come close to grasping the absolute, or, at least the possibility of the absolute existing.

It is said in the original teachings of most spiritual traditions and religions that creation is all one; "God" is everywhere and consciousness is all there is. Relative existence or duality is just an illusion – the illusion of Maya. Well, this is all well and good, but while we are in the middle of it, it's almost impossible, nay, completely impossible, to grasp such a concept. The mind fights and fights to regain its individuality: "No, I know I'm here and you are there – we can't all be one! It doesn't make sense!"

Well, look at it this way: In a dream, you often dream about other people and other objects, but you are still yourself, albeit not the physical version, but still a point of reference looking at these other people and objects. However, when you wake up, you know that you were in a dream. But how many people ever consider that the other people in the dream and the other objects were also themselves? Who else could they be? Nobody else can get into your dream, can they? The monster chasing you was... you!

Ok, we'll take it a step further. Imagine if that's actually what's happening when we're awake. Is it possible that we create our own universe? It's almost impossible to grasp, isn't it? You can sort of get it, but then it slips away. Looking for the truth in that is about as useful as running around in your dream looking for the body in the bed that's dreaming the dream. It can't be done, but it doesn't make it any less real that there is a body in a bed dreaming the dream.

But who is dreaming us while we're awake? That is the question, and when you grasp it, you have the pure source of all healing, for we can create health... or indeed ill health... in an instant. So, pay attention to your dreaming. It might just be the key to perfect health, and so much beyond!

Conclusion

My take on autoimmunity is that it is triggered from a much deeper level before it gets into the physiology and becomes a diagnosable illness. It probably comes from a combination of all manner of stresses, false beliefs, uncomfortable emotions, resentments against others and against oneself, childhood traumas... the list goes on and on and will be different for everybody. Finding the deep causes is actually the real fun of it. It becomes great detective work leading to blissful revelations and eventual resolutions. So why do some people remain healthy with more stress than it takes to break others? Well, that's a very complicated question down to numerous factors, but gleaned from my own experience I have a theory that I have never heard anyone else come up with, and it is this: A healthy body comes from a good gut protecting us from bad emotions. I'm sure it's not quite as simple as that, but it seems that when the gut flora/integrity is compromised and the body starts to break down, the symptoms linked to the emotions get worse. It's almost as if our immune system is not only there to protect us from external influences, but also from the destructive power of our own emotions. This is why it seems that the symptoms lessen dramatically when we fix the gut with diet and other methods, but never totally resolve until the deeper issues are addressed.

This is an amazing journey to go on, which can take you to levels of health and understanding of yourself that you never dreamed of.

Illness truly is a gift if we learn to see it like that.

The bigger the cloud, the bigger the potential silver lining.

PART THREE
The Nature of the Beast

⮑ CHAPTER 10
FIRST AWAKENING

Welcome to the third part of the book. This is the bit I've been looking forward to writing. In this part I'm going to cover some new areas and also some of the events I've already described, but from a totally different perspective, which is much easier to see in hindsight. Being so ill allowed me to look at many phases of my life and eventually make sense of them, some even decades after they happened. This part of the book is all about the deep-seated stresses that cause illness – the types that often start to form at the emotional and spiritual levels years before they manifest as a problem in the physiology. The blessing of illness is that it forces you to look at these deeper issues, and in doing so you not only have the ability to cure the incurable, but to discover your true essential nature and stabilise that experience so the universe becomes a beautiful and satisfying place – far better in fact than before you got ill. Well, of course the universe was always a wonderful place; you just didn't notice.

I am only writing this section of the book because I was so stupid that I ignored all those problems until they were magnified by the consciousness shifts I am about to describe and by my own stupidity. I sincerely believe that everyone can get to the root of their own false beliefs and damaging emotions without letting them go as far as I did. I just hope my experience, being a little larger than life will make it easier to shine a light on your own similar problems and issues so you can deal with them before they cause so much pain as they did to me.

Then again, many of you reading this book will already be in some extensive pain, in which case I hope this section inspires you to look at the magic of your situation instead of just getting bogged down in the suffering and losing faith.

Now that we have established that a contributing factor to autoimmunity is the manifestation in the body of decades of not loving what is (to oversimplify somewhat), let's look at how it develops. So where did all this fear and not loving what is come from in me? I will recount how it unfolded so maybe you can make parallels in your own lives.

It was late 1979, I was 17 years old, and I was hitchhiking back to my parents' house in Langley, near London, from Borth in Wales with my then partner, Katie. I had spent a fair amount of that autumn staying in a friend's caravan in the heart of magic mushroom territory where we could go out into the local fields and pick hundreds if not thousands of psilocybin mushrooms per day. We were tripping almost every day, and for me it was serious research into consciousness – this was no recreation. I had read the Carlos Castaneda books, and basically I wanted to be a sorcerer. I can't quite remember why we were coming back together or why I hadn't got my motorcycle... I think I'd actually had enough and decided to call it quits for the winter. It had been a heavy time. Katie hadn't been part of the tripping marathon; she had only come out to visit for a while at the end of the season, and I hadn't actually taken any mushrooms for some time prior to this journey home.

We had accepted a ride from a kind chap to a service station where we were meeting a good friend of ours, Mick Crocker. I was sitting in the front seat, and Katie was in the back seat when suddenly my world fell apart. It kind of felt like the start of a trip, but much more sudden. I felt myself dissolving, and I panicked. It was an awful feeling of losing myself, or so I interpreted it, because I just related it back to tripping and assumed it was a flashback... Of course it might very well have been a flashback on one level, but to me that doesn't make it any less valid, as the play of consciousness also goes on when there are drugs or drug effects involved. Ask any shaman!

I totally panicked and resisted it. I tried to grab wildly for myself to drag the parts of myself back together that I felt were drifting away. I was scared of descending into utter madness. I was flooded with adrenaline and in a state of complete terror.

I waited until we got to the service station before I tried to explain it to Katie, but how does one explain something like that? She was concerned, but I could not have expected her to understand. I was so scared I remember I had to go to the toilet, and as I sat there in the cubicle the door was melting and pulsating. What the hell had I done to myself? Mick turned up soon after, and I tried to explain to him what had happened too. Mick had been a big part of all the tripping and perhaps understood better, but being of a different character, he was not one of those prone to paranoia or flashbacks, so it was unlikely he could totally grasp what was going on.

I don't remember how we actually got home, but I do remember that life was never the same again. Every morning I'd wake up and things would look normal for a second, but then I'd remember that something was very wrong, and I'd start to panic, sometimes even leading to hallucinating mildly. It was a feeling of constant resistance... the total opposite to surrender that made the same experience so beautiful later in 2006. As I look back now, it seems utterly insane that I didn't welcome the dissolution of the ego (or more precisely expansion beyond the ego) with open arms and fall into it with unconditional love. Instead I freaked out about it intensely for about three years, and it then went on to dog me for almost another thirty in various subtle ways.

The continuing battle day-to-day was that I felt I was going to slip into an abyss, somewhere where I'd encounter the deepest levels of hell and insanity. I would have crippling panic attacks, which would result in constant adrenaline and chest pain to the point that it turned me into a hypochondriac. It must have been such a stress to my system that it caused so many physical symptoms.

There was nowhere to turn. None of my friends had experienced any adverse effects from hallucinogenics and were puzzled by my condition. I knew a regular doctor would be no good, but eventually my father said he would take me to a psychiatrist that had been recommended. My father said this doc had experience with people who had developed problems after taking drugs, so with small hope I agreed. Anyway, we went to Harley Street in London, and were met with the sight of an eccentric looking chap with a tweed suit, waistcoat, pocketwatch and little round glasses. He told me that I clearly had a drug-induced psychosis and that it might or might not go away. I should avoid any psychoactive drugs forever and also avoid countries where I might be likely to catch any tropical disease or similar that might put me into a feverish state, because that might also exaggerate the condition. He offered to prescribe some pills to calm me down, but I declined, thinking that since drugs had got me into this mess in the first place, I didn't really want to take any more. I left totally downhearted. Was that really the best advice modern medicine could give? I truly was on my own with this.

It was not until 2014 when listening to a Buddha at the Gas Pump interview with a Dr Robert Gersten that I realised what had happened to me is actually reasonably common. Since his own awakening in 1976, Gersten has been helping people who have misidentified an awakening and consequently suffered some sort of breakdown or psychosis. He talked about just how many people are in psychiatric hospitals being treated with drugs to lessen the effects when really what they need is the correct type of spiritual guidance and reassurance that the shift they have had is okay and to stop panicking. The idea that somebody on the planet back then knew exactly what was going on with me made me remember just what I would have given to be able to consult with him and be told that with a little surrender, it was actually a very precious and valuable shift, not the descent into madness that it seemed... Ah well, I guess my path was not destined to be so easy...

The condition raged on. It was a constant state of resistance to what is. I was caught in the senseless cycle of "fear of fear" almost constantly throughout the day. There was nothing concrete I was afraid of, but I was always worried that the fear I was feeling would get worse in the next few seconds/minutes and I'd descend into hell. It was a very strange way to live. There was no joy in anything; at best the world felt grey, a bleak, lifeless place, and at worst a nightmare of hell fire. I could not maintain a relationship with Katie, who I'd actually loved dearly previously, because my emotions seemed to have been wiped out, leaving only room for the fear and the resistance towards the fear, so we split up soon after that.

Perhaps at this point I should go into what led up to the mushroom tripping in Wales and why it hit me so hard. Earlier that year I had attended the Reading Rock Festival where I had tried my first LSD. It was very powerful and very blissful – eighteen hours solid of everything I had ever dreamed of being possible or feeling. I had spectacular hallucinations and both hilarious and magnificently expansive experiences, but beyond that, I came down from the trip with the distinct impression that there was a god. I didn't even know exactly what I meant by that, but I had definitely touched the essence of something. It took me back to my childhood when I used to have episodes in lessons while looking out of the window and daydreaming. I used to get momentary glimpses of what I used to call "the everything all at once". Suddenly, for a split second, the universe would open up, and I'd almost grasp it... but then it would slip from me, and I'd be left thinking desperately, "What was that? Why can't I remember?" Of course we cannot grasp it at all with the rational mind, so all my efforts to recall it were thwarted... until the next time I got a tiny glimpse through the veil.

That first acid trip in Reading though had taken me back there and dumped me securely in that territory for many hours. In fact my first ever experience on the first ever trip was a lovely demonstration of universal mind. We were sitting in a large tent belonging to a biker friend of one of us, and there were four of us if I remember correctly, waiting for the LSD to start working. I had no idea what to expect, so I was looking for the familiar, a drunk or stoned feeling that I was used to. Nothing of the sort became apparent, so I assumed it wasn't working. Another of the bikers came into the tent and kicked over a large jerry can used for petrol. We all recoiled as the petrol spilled out over the floor of the tent, and the smell was overpowering as it splashed onto us. We were also smoking cigars that we had been given for some reason, and we all quickly lifted them out of the way. I remember thinking I was going to be burned alive. It was only when somebody pointed out that not only was the can empty, but the lid was screwed on tightly, that we realised that the acid was indeed working, and that we had all just shared a crystal clear vision.

From then on, researching into that state and pursuing higher consciousness was all I cared about. Any thoughts of a career or money (few as they ever had been) vanished, and I even put my worldly loves of drumming and carp fishing onto the backburner.

That autumn, we all decided to move to Borth in Wales, hole up in a friend's caravan (or "trailer" for the benefit of any US readers) and take massive amounts of psilocybin mushrooms, up to hundreds per day. From then on, I never had a really good trip again. I mean, I could recount a hundred hilarious and bizarre experiences that would make it sound like I was having the time of my life, but I never managed to surrender like I did in that first trip at Reading in the summer. The memory of the really bad trip was still never far from my mind, but that didn't stop me taking some mega doses and having some very far out experiences.

However, all this "teetering" taught me fear; in fact I became a connoisseur, so I am not surprised that it culminated in the experience while hitching back from Wales. I really put myself through the wringer. All through my childhood I had been happy and carefree on the surface, but I suppose I must have always had this tendency to resist situations. Hallucinogenics cannot cause mental problems, but they can certainly amplify what is already potentially there.

At this point some of you might be wondering how all this tripping stuff is relevant to you, and that I'm just some old hippy who mashed his brain and went mad, and it doesn't have any bearing on the progression of autoimmune disease... Well, please bear with me...

There is always some sort of trigger that brings out our inner demons. It can be a traumatic life event, bereavement, childhood abuse or even just a steady accumulation of life's stresses from always kicking against what's happening. There are many and varied ways that the mind battles reality, as many as there are people who experience such a thing, so it will be up to you to look for your own stresses that might be at the root of any problems you have. I'm merely recounting my experiences to demonstrate how one person learned to fear the universe and eventually manifest that fear in his joints.

I often wonder what life would have been like had I just left it after that first trip, savouring the memory of the blissful, expansive trip I'd had in Reading without ever having to know what a bad trip was like. Then I could have pursued my experiments in consciousness with something gentler and more natural such as TM... It might have been a far easier few years, but then again I'll never know. However, now I am very grateful for it, as the combination of experiences probably led me to where I am now. Without a good solid dark side, there is often no compensating swing of the pendulum to the positive.

Oddly, I also attended a TM intro talk back then, but the fact that it seemed to me to be more for businessmen with migraines than the serious researcher into consciousness that I considered myself to be put me off. Also the chap in the suit giving the intro talk put me off too, as my guru wouldn't be dressed like a bank manager; he'd sport ten-foot dreadlocks, a loincloth and appear in a flash of blinding white light... wouldn't he? So, I decided to give meditating a miss and fill myself full of mushrooms instead. I got around to meditating in the end of course, but it took a few more years.

During those couple of years when I really wrestled with the full force of that psychotic state, I often had the thought that even if I cured myself, it would end up returning when I was around 50. Whether this was an actual premonition or a self-fulfilling prophecy is impossible to say, but return it did (when I was 48, so I wasn't far off), but not how I imagined. By that time of course, it was raging in the physiology, not the mind, although it took me another two years or so to make the connection and see that it was very closely related to the more cerebral problems of 30 years previously. It is also rather interesting that in 2011, when I was very ill, Mick Crocker found me through my website and contacted me again after all those years. It was so lovely to see him again. He is still throwing himself into life with his beautiful brand of open surrender, and he was a great help and inspiration to me during the years I was finding my way out of my mess. Isn't life magical if we just take notice of it?

So, for a year or so after the mushroom tripping, it was full-on, and some aspect of it took over pretty much every second of every day, colouring in other experiences. Anything that caused any fear at all had to be avoided, even the "recreational" fear of a frightening film for example. I did not enjoy a good healthy scare any longer because any fear that started in me ended up falling into the territory of actual psychosis. The strangest one was that I could not even look at a starry night sky. The sheer vastness triggered a massive wave of fear and adrenaline as I associated it with the internal abyss I was always so scared of losing myself in. It was obvious all I wanted to do was contract – I was scared of letting go in every respect. Externally I wasn't a gibbering wreck by any means; I went about my life, and most people never knew there was a problem, but internally it was all a massive tumult.

In 1983 I learned Transcendental Meditation and then in 1986 I did the advanced TM-Sidhi programme including the residential flying course. Even from the very start I had wonderful expansive and blissful experiences meditating, and they increased and intensified as time went on. Also from the very start it helped greatly in calming down any of the aftereffects of the tripping, and I started to feel much more sane. I can see now though that I was still resisting. I would fall into what is known in the TM circles as "the transcendent", the subtlest state of mind (or beyond mind), but I would pull back instead of totally surrendering. I still felt there was some sort of abyss I might disappear into, as I had got so used to that ridiculous mind-pattern over the previous few years. This meant that I would have small panic attacks during meditation – nothing like they used to be, but little episodes of adrenaline here and there, maybe three or four during a 20-minute meditation. It seems insane to me now that I was actually resisting the very thing that would probably have totally cured what was left of the old psychosis!

Around that time, among my avid devouring of all books on Indian saints and their lives, I read one called "Kundalini" by Gopi Krishna, which was probably the worst thing I could have done. It is the story of how he had a full kundalini experience while meditating one morning, but it all went horribly wrong. For those unfamiliar with kundalini, it is supposed to be the dormant serpent energy that lies coiled in the muladhara (root) chakra and when stirred up by spiritual practice of some sort, rises through the intermediate chakras to merge with the sahasrara (highest) chakra on the crown of the head. Tradition says that it should go up the sushumna, the central channel, but sometimes it can go up the channels either side, called ida or pingala. I forget which "wrong" channel the energy took in poor old Gopi, but after a blissful meditation and lots of white light as it reached sahasrara, he ended his meditation and realised that something was wrong. There followed 19 years of fiery hell until he finally got it to go up sushumna and all was finally well (sorry for the spoiler, guys). He described the state he was in over those years, and it had a lot of similarities to my own state since that fateful magic mushroom season.

Of course this made me frightened of even meditating in case it made my condition worse. I remember one day, I got to the part in the meditation programme where I was doing a particular "sutra", which is a technique taught as part of the sidhi course. Suddenly I was in a burning, raging hell and opened my eyes, terrified that something had gone wrong, Gopi Krishna-style. That day I couldn't even finish my meditation. The next day, the same thing happened again, but this time I got through it, and it passed as I moved on to the other sutras. After a few days it was still happening, and I was not enjoying my meditations at all; I was even thinking of giving up, which devastated me as I thought it was my saviour, and I had even made it my life. What would I do without it?

Some days later, as I came to that sutra, the feeling of being in a burning hell was particularly strong, and I was in total despair. I was just too tired to fight it anymore, so I decided I'd had enough; I would surrender and throw myself into the fiery abyss. I just didn't care; I wanted all this nonsense to stop, and if it meant going completely insane and burning up in hell, then so be it. I could not resist it any longer. Sitting there with my eyes closed, I looked at the flaming monster and just threw myself into it, completely letting go... and yes... you guessed it... I found out that the abyss does not exist at all. Instead there was just peace and bliss. I cried with relief and joy, but afterwards I was a little sad as the realisation hit me that all the fear I had experienced since 1979 had just been of my own making, and one act of true surrender would more than likely have ended all my problems. Never again did I have any problems meditating, but those few years did leave me with something more subtle and sinister that did eventually lead to my body attacking itself. It left me in a subtle state of not loving what is. Perhaps if I had not been so overjoyed at seeing the back of the baseless panic attacks, I might have noticed that I resisted almost every aspect of my life on a subtle level, but because the abject fear had gone, I seemed as though I was healed. It had taken away the acute phase of the problem, but had left me with a chronic, niggling set of beliefs and reactions that were hard to identify for an emotionally immature 24-year-old.

As I look back to my life over the next 24 years until the arthritis really struck, I can see almost nothing but resistance. I was always looking for something better – a new possession, a new lover and even the spiritual materialism that so many get caught up in – better experiences, more advanced techniques etc. I would also get subtly irritated at almost everything, from what somebody had said about me to inanimate objects not obeying me, such as cutlery being difficult to pick up from a drawer. I was constantly fighting life on all levels, but I just didn't seem to notice. After all, I was an advanced meditator, a true yogi, so what did I need to look at in myself? I was on the path to perfection... wasn't I? It is a trap that many spiritual people get caught in, thinking that because they have some sort of tradition, technique, or even religion, they are somehow above the things that affect mere mortals. This can stop a great deal of useful work being undertaken on their emotions and false beliefs that would probably do them far more good than sitting and meditating or praying. Now, I'm not knocking meditation and would recommend anyone who has never tried it to go and learn immediately, but it is a tool to experience peace and maybe even a glimpse of the absolute; it is not the answer to all your problems on every level, so keep it in perspective.

This is the main problem with organised spirituality of any

sort in my opinion. If it's misunderstood it can be a dangerous obstacle that can have you treading water for decades while mistakenly thinking you are on the righteous path and all is well. It can be very difficult to turn back from such a dead end of ingrained beliefs, and it can often provoke some pretty angry reactions should you suggest it to anyone so encumbered. It's a realisation that one has to come to for oneself, and it is this very realisation that I am most grateful to arthritis for bringing to me.

Speaking of arthritis, it is easy for me to look back now and see that certain of my more ingrained and common emotional blocks and false beliefs caused the stirrings of my arthritic genetics way before it hit me full force. I had periods of inflammation in my feet and Achilles tendons twice in my life: once when I was having problems in my marriage around the early 90s and once when I was having a very hard time in a volatile relationship around 1999 to 2003. This was pretty similar in energy to the problems I had with living with my mother around 2010 when my ankles really blew up. Each time it got slightly worse than the previous time, as if the body was saying, "I warned you before... now listen to me this time!" It really was the same feeling of trying not to run away from a bad situation each time. Was it a coincidence that exactly the same area of my body became affected each time? I think not. Try telling that to a rheumatologist though.

Also around the time of my marriage breakup, I also had trouble with my wrist starting to hurt a lot. This was never diagnosed back then, but it seems interesting that it was around the time that I was also having trouble with my "reach exceeding my grasp". Similarly, trouble I have had with my knees over the years have always been at times when I felt I was "not moving forward in life", just as the text books (Hay/Segal etc) say will happen. I am utterly convinced that this is the process with physical illness as it manifests from the subtler levels of emotions.

I urge anybody reading this to really look at themselves and discover the magic of how clearing emotional blocks can lead to the end of the related physical issue. It's wonderful to see it in action! It took me a long time to see the regular patterns that were making me ill repeatedly, and then a few months to clear the major blocks that I had.

The main one for me was as I describe in an upcoming chapter when I look at my tendency to always want to help and fix people. How the universe changed when I let go of that rubbish! This also allowed me to see that I had been controlling and manipulative in so many ways over the years. People had told me too, but I never really understood. I always meant well – helping people out financially if they showed an interest in starting a business maybe, or even roping people into big projects such as bands etc when perhaps they did not totally share my dream. I meant well and loved helping and supporting, so I never saw that this was a problem, but I did upset people, and then when I had to deal with that upset, it sent me down the old track of: "Poor me – I was only trying to help; they should be more grateful, the bastards…"

Almost without exception if you are using "should" or "should not" you are probably talking absolute crap. This is a clear example of not accepting a situation for what it is, and once you notice it, it can be a very useful marker for something that you need to work on.

It is also very often a marker for blame. Blaming others for misfortunes that we suffer is a big obstacle that almost all of us run into at some time and to varying extents during our lives. The people with the most serious health complaints almost always have this trait; I see it all the time. They often blame somebody else for every single little thing that happens to them. Letting go of the ridiculous belief that it's necessary to change people and/or harbour grudges for perceived wrongs is one of the most liberating, healing and transformative processes one can go through.

I watch with horror these days the pain and blame that goes on in couples who have split up. The "he said/she said" cycle of blame is painful to listen to, and it can go on for a long time. I have been guilty of it myself in the past, and it's such a huge stress to be thinking such appalling things of somebody who you once loved deeply. If we could only realise that life brings pain, and pain is part of growing and evolving, so we need to surrender and ride it to where it's taking us, not blame somebody else for it being there in the first place. What a wasted opportunity for evolving!

All the time we are blaming others, we have no chance of resolving the issues that are actually causing our pain because we don't see that they are all of our own creation. Once we can see that we are the architects of our own hells, we are well on the way to dismantling those hells. One of the most useful abilities a person can have is the ability to look at themselves honestly and say, "What a complete idiot I am!"

So these are the events that led up to my own resistance to life, which I feel sure led to my own body resisting itself (autoimmunity). This was my own series of life events that sent me off the rails. In your own life you may not be able to see yet what the big issues are, and my advice would be don't dig for them. They may be buried under a load of apparent smaller issues, so just deal with the problems you are facing today, right at this very moment. Get familiar with any emotional clearance technique that appeals to you, and get right onto all those niggling little issues and unwind them. Make it your hobby, zapping those daft thoughts constantly as you go through each day, hundreds of times if you can. Really install that software properly! Then one day you might just hit the mother lode and unlock a massive knot of old stresses, taking you right to the root of a major life stress that you perhaps didn't even know was there. Believe me, you'll know when you hit it!

◯ CHAPTER 11
SECOND AWAKENING

It was one balmy evening in the summer of 2006, and I was outside in the back garden of my house in Skelmersdale, smoking a cigarette (yes, my healthy lifestyle had well and truly degenerated) and pondering the feelings of guilt I had been having about not going into the "Dome" (a nearby purpose built meditation centre) to meditate regularly. As I let my eyes wander around the garden, suddenly everything I thought I knew about the universe collapsed, and I sat down on the low wall that surrounded the lawn or I would probably have fallen over. But let me explain how I ended up there in the first place...

In 1986 when I was 24, I moved to Skelmersdale, a small northern town in the UK about halfway between Liverpool and Manchester, partially taken over by the TM (Transcendental Meditation) movement in the 1970s. I had moved from a privileged upbringing in the affluent counties of Surrey and Berkshire in the south to be a yogi and to meditate and "fly" morning and evening in the Dome until I got enlightened. That was the idea, anyway.

I had learned the Transcendental Meditation technique of Maharishi Mahesh Yogi (the so-called Beatles' guru) in 1982, and I'd gone on to do the advanced TM-Sidhi course in 1986, a collection of techniques taken from Patanjali's ancient Yoga Sutras, which famously include the "flying sidhi" (sidhi meaning power) where people hop around on foam mattresses cross-legged or in lotus position, attempting to fly while in a meditative state. The theory is that it brings the transcendent, or deeper level of meditation, into activity, thus allowing one to experience higher states of consciousness in everyday life. I had been a totally dedicated practitioner of this for several years after I moved to Skelmersdale, but by the mid to late 90s I was losing interest. My meditations became sporadic, and I hardly ever bothered to fly at all.

After my father died in 2003, I moved back to Skelmersdale in 2004 from a nearby town and bought a house near the Dome. I also had the idea that it was time to get fit and healthy again after letting things slide, and I resolved to get back into the Dome to replenish myself spiritually as well. However, by 2006 I had only walked the 50 yards or so to go and meditate in the group two or three times in total, so it was clear that my heart wasn't in it anymore.

I didn't realise, but I had some guilt about this, almost in the same way as religious people feel guilty when they lose their faith, but that day in the back garden, half-smoked rollup in hand, I saw the guilt for what it was at last, and I decided that if I wasn't interested anymore, I should just let it go and stop letting it bother me.

So that's what I did... I totally let go of the idea of myself as a spiritual person, as the yogi I'd always thought of myself as. I let that persona fall away, and all expectations of ever getting "enlightened" along with it. It was a huge chunk of myself to lose.

It's funny how sometimes such seemingly inconsequential events can alter everything, because that was the moment the whole universe changed for me. In letting go of the quest, in dropping my seeking, I suddenly saw what it was that I had been seeking all along. I saw that it had always been there, mostly hidden by the seeking itself. I knew nothing would ever be the same again, and I could barely stand up. I dropped down and sat down while I tried to make sense of what had happened.

Now, how to explain what actually happened that day? Do I have any chance of putting into words what so many have tried and failed to do down the ages? I doubt it, but I'll still have a go...

In that moment I saw that all my seeking for enlightenment, all the chasing of more and more powerful spiritual experiences was actually a load of extraneous nonsense and a very powerful distraction from what has always been right in front of me, all around me and inside me. I had been under the misapprehension, as so many meditators and seekers are, that there is something spectacular to gain, that one day this little individual person will attain some sort of godlike status, and freedom, happiness and bliss will descend in bucketfuls from the sky. Then again, although I was pursuing it, I still didn't ever 100% believe I would attain it... at least not in this lifetime. Spiritual enlightenment was the domain of Indian saints and sages... the older, the more unattainable and the more dead the better, and the greater the sage. It just didn't happen to ordinary people... did it?

And yet, there it was... I was sitting on that wall reeling from the fact that one moment of pure surrender had given me what twenty-five years of meditation had failed to. In looking for an experience I had failed to notice that what I was looking for was not an experience at all. Instead, it is just noticing the simple, plain fact that this... right here... right now is "IT"... all we ever need. It was so utterly simple, so utterly perfect and so downright fucking obvious. I started to laugh. I was reminded of another great sage, Ramana Maharshi's quote, and I paraphrase: "At the moment of enlightenment, you will laugh at all your efforts to get there."

I laughed because I finally saw that it's not about attaining anything; it's about subtracting the limiting beliefs that keep up the illusion that we are all separate beings. At that moment I saw the totality of everything and how I fitted into it. I saw myself as part of the whole cosmic computer, a tiny cog in the machine that is the universe. And finally, I was content with that. In that moment the ego character Phil lost a great deal of his hold on how I see myself, or rather as the universe sees things through these "borrowed" eyes that are set in this lump of flesh.

Looking back, it was basically the exact same experience that I had in that car in 1979, but unlike that time, I managed to surrender. However, I see that this was still just a partial realisation, because I was still Phil, just a little dissolved... but at least I saw myself as part of the whole. I did not stop to consider that I might have some way to go yet – I was sorted... done... it was all over! Like the impulsive idiot I have been for most of my life, over the next few weeks, I jumped straight onto another misapprehension, that there is just one moment when you wake up once and for all, and I decided that it had happened to me and threw myself right into the first and most ugly effect of an awakening – letting the ego take it over and run with it.

I became a nightmare! I didn't exactly shout it from the rooftops, but I did pester my friends and family, especially the meditating ones. I would tell them that spiritual practice is not necessary, and that all one needs is a moment of surrender for realisation to dawn. This might be ultimately true, but there is usually some considerable (if illusory) "path" leading to that realisation, and it's probably impossible to cut that path short, especially by challenging people's beliefs when they haven't even asked. It's no wonder some got annoyed. I was lucky that my partner and most of my good friends who I mentioned it to put up with it, but I did lose a few. I encountered quite a bit of disbelief and hostility too, even among those close to me, which surprised me, because if somebody had told me about such a thing, I would have been fascinated.

After that day in the back garden I had a sort of honeymoon period for a few months. Life was bliss. I even reacted to my yogi years by going against all of the recommended spiritual and moral practices in a festival of rebellion. I have always been a rebel, and taking up TM and moving to the TM community was rebellious in many ways to my previous life, but now I stupidly even felt some hostility towards TM and wanted to rebel against that, believing that I had wasted all those years when all I needed to do was let go. I started to drink alcohol and even smoke ganja from time to time, just trying to prove that the state I had attained was nothing to do with being all pure, abstaining from stimulants and eating a vegetarian diet. I wanted to test this awakening with as much depravity as I could.

I had had a glimpse of the absolute for sure, and certain aspects of that realisation had stayed with me, but ever the idiot, I without doubt abused the gift I had been given. Just after my experience in the garden, I telephoned Roger Linden, an ex-director of the TM community in Skelmersdale, and now an awakened teacher in London. He was the only one who I could think of who might have had such an awakening and who was reasonably accessible and approachable. He was very helpful and told me that it sounded like I had had a genuine shift, but it might take a long time to stabilise it, maybe even ten years, so not to get too cocky about it. It's easy to see one's mistakes in hindsight, but at the time my world had been turned so dramatically upside down that it was hard to realise and admit that my behaviour was a bit off to say the least.

Roger did, however, point me in the direction of Tony Parsons, a very uncompromising non-dual teacher from the UK who he said had been an influence on his own awakening. Watching his talks on YouTube, and others like him with a similar (if slightly less uncompromising) message such as Adyashanti, Mooji, Rupert Spira etc, they started to make a lot of sense and seemed to mirror the experience I'd had more than the long, drawn-out process of decades of meditation finally culminating in some realisation. What had happened to me seemed so much simpler and more instant, and the more non-dual based people I was watching confirmed that.

I developed an aversion to anything traditionally spiritual or guru-based. I'd mock the strictness of spiritual people's lifestyles and their devotion to some man or woman on a podium in front of them who they really believed could take them to freedom. This giving away of one's power seemed to be the most ridiculous waste of time, and the fact that I had been guilty of it for so long added to that my growing horror of it. Maybe I had had a little peek into what is, but at the time I was certainly not loving what is on many levels. I was on the right track in a way, but taking it so personally and really worrying about it was definitely adding to my stress, which finally added up and took me out of my honeymoon period.

However, I still had access to that realm in my quieter moments and could see my place in the universe quite clearly. If I sat still for a while the bliss and peace would pour over me far more powerfully than when I had meditated regularly, even though I'd always had good experiences.

In 2005 I'd also compounded my stresses by deciding to become a businessman – more specifically a property developer/landlord when I was really more artistic by temperament. It went against the grain, but I was flying through the money I had saved and decided that I needed to find a way to make the money grow and set up a passive income, which I did by starting a property business in Ireland with some friends. They lived out there and did the actual work while I signed cheques and spoke to solicitors. This went okay until Ireland's economy collapsed and we had to pull out in a hurry. Detta and I started to buy property in Liverpool and soon built a small portfolio of six houses, which we rented out. I remember in 2008/2009 the whole process caused me a lot of stress, but I thought I was invincible due to my awakening.

At this point I'd like to stress that I felt enormously grateful for my easy financial life; I just managed it incorrectly. I got swept up in what I thought I should do, trying to multiply my finances, instead of just sitting back and using it to support my artistic and musical endeavours that were so close to my heart. Go against your essential nature and your passion and even a seemingly great gift can become a curse. I was also incredibly grateful for that money when I was very ill, as it enabled me to do such a massive amount of research and experimentation that would not have been possible if I'd had a regular nine to five job. My dissatisfaction was with myself for how I handled it.

My daughter Amelia was also born in 2008, and although this was another true gift, it took me a few years to fully realise that too. At the time I saw it as a scary responsibility that didn't fit with my new pompous role as one of the awakened, and so it created added pressure. So, with the combination of a dreadful diet, alcohol, cigarettes, ganja, trying to be a businessman, being frightened of my own child and still very resentful towards my mother, it's no wonder it created the perfect storm to usher in serious illness by the end of 2010. Looking back, I am amazed my body held up for as long as it did. In my quest to prove that awakening had nothing to do with any of the conventional methods to get there, and actively testing it with abusing my body and my emotions, I finally landed myself in proper trouble.

On top of this, my music wasn't going too well, as I was distracted by the property business, and I was starting to have conflicts with one of my bandmates. We just didn't seem to be able to agree on anything, and it hurt to see my beloved friendship and project slip away, owing to what I felt were misunderstandings and trivialities.

In 2009 I decided to really make an effort to get back on track. I started the website pureactivity.net to track my progress back to health. I was overweight and suffered from a lot of niggling ailments that I have already listed in part one. I rewrote some of the Pure Activity book I'd written back in 1996 to sell it as an e-book and started blogging openly about how I had neglected my health and fitness, but now I was eating more healthily (or so I mistakenly thought at the time) and getting back into mountain biking and weight training etc. I was surprised that I was seeing little or no progress; in fact I was getting worse, and then, a year or so later, it all went horribly wrong. This was distressing enough, but was now actually embarrassing because I had a health website. What a fraud I am, I thought to myself.

So, we are now up to the autumn of 2010, and we arrive back at the place where part one of this book started, when my joints blew up in a riot of inflammation. In trying to prove that the awakening was unshakeable however much abuse one threw at it, here I was in such pain, such hell, that the experience of it finally covered up any awakening I might have had, and all I could think of all day long was the suffering I had landed myself in. Not that I realised I had landed myself in it at the time; I blamed anyone and anything apart from my own stupidity. I also revelled in victim mode, wondering how on Earth I had fallen from grace so spectacularly. I felt I had been robbed of heaven, and I blamed and blamed and blamed doctors, my mother, the TM movement, the Hindus for their bad diet advice, Detta for wanting kids... anyone but myself. I wasn't very nice to be around.

Here's my take on it now: Yes, it's possible to have all sorts of problems after an apparent awakening; in fact such an awakening might very well precipitate a lot of problems and intensify them so you have no choice but to face them so you can solve the puzzles they bring.

And so I came back into the body with a bump. Looking back, I was so mistaken that I had to make some sort of a choice between my realisation and my body, but at the time it felt like that. I figured I needed to forget all that airy fairy stuff and get my physiology sorted, so the fight began, and the horrors described in the first part of this book unfolded.

Of course I didn't need to take that path. Ideally I would have thanked the universe for the gift it had brought me and relaxed into it, letting the solutions wash over me in their own time. Actually, it feels more like watching yourself through the eyes of the universe. Seeing what happens to your own body is often no more personal than what happens to somebody else's body when a shift of consciousness has happened. However, I felt so panicked about the awful pain my body was in that I thought I had to give it total attention and force myself back into it. This was a mistake, but an inevitable one.

As the pain took hold and I became almost confined to the sofa for long periods, I spent my time researching on the Internet for many hours a day and meditating again out of desperation. It felt like a step back, but in the manner of people who pray only when they need something, I hoped that meditating might unlock some sort of magic that would suddenly heal all my joints up. Actually, it was interesting, as when I did meditate and put my attention on the affected joints, the feeling in them would turn from agony to an almost unbearable bliss. This made me think I was getting somewhere, but I wasn't really. It just shows that any experience is just that – an experience. Anything that has an opposite is not the true reality. I was back on the hamster wheel of thinking that if I did something (meditation) I would get something (healing) at some indeterminate time in the future. This kept me stuck in the state I was in, and since the meditation didn't seem to work, I became obsessed with diet, which I have already covered.

Sometime in 2011 a good friend visited and recommended that I look into something deeper than diet. He told me about the book "The Healing Code", which I went and bought immediately. I looked at it halfheartedly without really taking it in. It was the first time I had ever really looked at so-called emotional issues and their role in triggering physical symptoms. It lists many root causes of various complaints, covering the whole spectrum of human emotions. Because I had spent so long as a yogi I mistakenly considered myself above it all.

I remember one day in the summer, taking some painkillers so I could go carp fishing for the night, specifically to study the book and get to grips with it. I filled out all the forms that are available on the website to find out your emotional imbalances, stayed up half the night reading all the corresponding chapters, and in the morning I was cross-eyed trying to make sense of it.

This is the frustrating part for me now when I advise people about how to investigate their own illness. I stress from very early on that they should look at emotional balancing, but I forget just how long it took me to understand what is actually involved in this process. There really is absolutely no use in just doing it halfheartedly, or in straining to dig up the past if it hasn't presented itself via a problem in the present. I struggled along, doing the exercises from The Healing Codes a couple of times a day here and there and tapping away EFT-style a few times a week, and although I felt a little temporary relief, it didn't really hit the spot or bring about any permanent change.

It wasn't until some time in 2012 when I started to have sessions with my great friend Meidi Goodson, practitioner of EFT/Reiki/NLP and many more, that I started to see what was involved. If you are at this stage in your own healing I heartily recommend that you go to see a skilled practitioner and let them show you how you can then take charge of your own emotional balancing. Otherwise you might grope around in the dark for a long time and fail, thus losing confidence in such things altogether and missing out on some real magic.

So, I slid back into terror, and my emotional and mental states through the time that I wrested with the joints and Lyme scare plus the hernia and kidney stone operations were at an all-time low. I was suicidal at times, but still oddly had access to the awareness that my awakening had revealed to me. It was ironic that I had finally discovered what I had sought all my life, but still wanted to kill myself due to the unremitting pain. Still this came from a loss, or at least a great lessening, of the fear of death. I wasn't all that fussed if I lived or not; I just wanted to be free of the pain, but in focusing on it, fighting it and wallowing in it, I made sure it stayed put. It's a difficult stage in any healing journey, and I have lots of sympathy for those who give up and seek out conventional medical care.

However much I resisted the need to clear some of the old emotions out, it was clear that it needed to be done, and Meidi was an enormous help in setting me on the right path. She showed me how to relax and let the answers come to me via whatever was showing up at the time. As I spoke to her in our sessions, it wasn't long before it became obvious that the issues I had with my mother were very deep-seated in me. I always used to talk about her in terms of "should have" or "shouldn't have": I should have put her in a home when I could and not wasted my forties looking after her... I should have gone off to India and not given up my life to make sure she was okay... She shouldn't be so emotionally closed, hostile and disapproving... She shouldn't pretend to be so helpless so people have to look after her... She shouldn't be so nasty to Detta... The nonsense went on and on, and Meidi spotted it pretty quickly.

On top of that I had other shoulds going on: I should have spent my father's money more wisely... The guys in the band should have understood my illness better and been more sympathetic... I should never have eaten a vegetarian diet for so long... I was even worrying that I should have stayed down south and never moved up north, which pretty much negated the past twenty-five years of my life. It was clear that although I had been given a perspective on my place in the cosmic computer, I was kicking against all aspects of my situation instead of loving all of my blessings.

I finished my sessions with Meidi, as I felt she had showed me exactly how to look at myself and clear these damaging emotions, and I set off on my own, very excited to get to grips with the nonsense in my head and clear it. I felt like I finally understood the path into this new level of healing, and devoured the knowledge voraciously in the same way as I had done with diet over the previous three years.

I looked at three main sources for ways to investigate: Firstly I looked at EFT, and eventually found Robert Smith's Faster EFT site where the hundreds of free videos of him working on people really resonated with me. I know that recently Faster EFT has fallen into some disrepute with the conventional EFT people, but I think both methods are valid. I care nothing for squabbles between factions of any discipline – everything is out there because it has a value for somebody. EFT might appeal to some and faster EFT to others – explore both, as they are both very useful. What I loved about Robert Smith was what an unconventional rebellious type he was. He spoke to my own rebellious nature, and I loved his sense of humour in the videos, even as he unwound very deep-seated issues in people – or more accurately, led them to unwind the issues for themselves. There are many videos on his website and YouTube, so check them out. In case you are unfamiliar with EFT, it involves tapping gently with the fingers on a series of acupressure points while at first accepting the issue you are dealing with (i.e. "Even though I […insert issue here…], I completely love and accept myself…") and then using various affirmations to unwind the issue. Robert Smith's method just cuts a few corners and is simpler.

Secondly, I discovered "The Work" of Byron Katie and her four simple questions to look at anything that's troubling you. The questions are: 1. Is it true? 2. Are you absolutely sure it's true? 3. How does that thought make you feel? 4. How would you feel without that thought? They reframe the thought totally and show that the problem is the thought, not anyone else or any external problem. This had me quickly wading through many problems that I was causing myself by, as she puts it, not loving what is.

Thirdly, I bought a book called "The Secret Language of the Body" by Inna Segal. It had been recommended by Robert Smith in one of his videos as "Louise Hay on steroids". Having read Louise Hay's book on relating physical symptoms to emotional causes, I was keen to see a more detailed look at this subject, and I wasn't disappointed. This is a gem of a book, and although her recommended methods of clearing these emotions are probably very useful to many, they didn't resonate with me, but her way of diagnosing them is very accurate. I preferred to diagnose with her book then use EFT and The Work to clear the problems. You can look up the part of the body that's troubling you, even down to individual vertebrae, and relate them back to deeper problems in the emotions/beliefs. Sometimes it's immediately accurate, and sometimes it takes sitting with it for a little while before you see a similar pattern in yourself, subtly different from what she suggests in the book... We are complicated individuals (on one level at least) after all.

I began working very hard. I took every false belief that I could find and tapped on it like mad and hit it with Byron Katie's four questions. I didn't do this a few times a day, but gave over pretty much my whole day to it, tapping when in private, and questioning when out and about. There was pretty much no time I wasn't working on myself, and the "shoulds" started to fall down like dominoes. I started to love everyone I knew for who and what they were – the resentments towards my mother vanished, and our relationship improved despite her still being the same old mum. My self-criticism about my actions and decisions went up on a puff of smoke too, and I even started to completely forgive those who I thought had wronged me in some way – a huge block for poor little me, the perpetual victim. I even totally forgave my body for causing me so much pain. I also fell in love with Detta and Amelia all over again and deeper than I could ever have imagined. I started to really appreciate my blessings.

It was so exciting to clear all of this old rubbish I had been holding onto for years, and as it retreated so did a lot more of the pain. Certain other joints started to heal up with no lasting damage, and I started to feel totally exhilarated with my progress. I wanted to shout about it to everyone. To me now it seemed so obvious why everyone was getting ill – they were eating rubbish that the government told them was healthy, and they were attacking themselves with false beliefs and entrenched emotional blocks. I needed to save the planet. I had discovered my vocation and was duty bound to pass on all these wonderful secrets. Nobody was safe from my evangelism. After all, it was okay to tell people about all this stuff, as I was helping, right? How could I have been so selfish, both indulging in my pain and ill health and also retreating into the ocean of consciousness after my previous awakening? How could I have thought that we are all part of one organism when paradoxically we are also individuals, and so many individuals were in pain and needed my help. I was mortified every time I saw the increasingly grey skin and muscle wastage on ageing vegetarian friends, and accosted them in the supermarket, lecturing them on diet until their eyes glazed over. Why didn't they listen? It was probably only because I have a reasonably charming manner about me that I wasn't punched in the face several times. I was a right pain in the arse, perhaps even worse than after my initial awakening.

And then disaster struck. Around the beginning of 2013 I awoke one morning with a pain in my left eye. I knew exactly what it was, having had prior experience three times. It was a bout of iritis – a painful inflammation of the iris that goes hand-in-hand with so many autoimmune problems. It is the one thing that I will seek conventional medical help for, as to ignore it can cause you to lose your sight. I had managed to turn one bout of the previous three around on my own by clearing an issue to do with my son, and I was pleased with that, as it's yet another thing that's supposed to be impossible, but even then I was one day away from going to the eye department at the hospital anyway.

This time I had no such luck figuring out what was going on, so I headed to the local hospital to get the steroid drops that provide blessed relief from the awful pain upon refocusing the eye that is characteristic of iritis.

I tipped the drops into the eye every hour, expecting relief by the second day, but none came. To cut a long story short, a couple of weeks later there wasn't much improvement; in fact things had taken a turn for the worse, and my central vision was becoming very dark and distorted. People's faces looked like demons, and I couldn't see road signs or print on the computer. I returned to the eye department where they told me that I had macular edema, a pooling of fluid under the macula. It's rare that iritis goes this far, and when it's in the macula it is a lot more potentially dangerous than just in the iris. I saw the concern on the faces of the doctors.

I was horrified. I mean, why should I suddenly get such a nasty problem when everything else was healing and going so well? I was totally deflated. Maybe everything I had done was for nothing, and now I was going to lose my sight as well. How cruel was this autoimmunity? How long was it going to punish me?

In desperation, I consulted Inna Segal's book and saw something I had missed – the problems with the eye could, she pointed out, be to do with seeing things that we don't like in our environment. I had thought that I had cleared a lot of the contributing factors to my eyes flaring up, and was at a loss for a while what it was that I wasn't loving, because I had done so much work on that.

Thinking my stupidity had potentially lost me my sight, I now redoubled my efforts with the EFT and The Work.

↻ Chapter 12
THIRD AWAKENING

One morning while still suffering with my failing eyesight, something occurred to me in a quiet moment. I remembered Meidi sitting in front of me at one of our last sessions, and she was saying, "Yes, but have they asked?" It was in response to my discourse on how I wanted to save everyone and tell them about diet and lifestyle changes. At the time I didn't really think it was a problem and laughed it off. After all, I had so many issues that were quite clearly negative, so I didn't really need to worry about my rabid concern for my fellow man, did I? That was a symptom of being a good, caring person, wasn't it? Surely it was one of my few positive traits!

By this time I had learned not to ignore any spontaneous thought, vision or dream that arose, so I pondered why that vision of Meidi asking that little question had popped into my head. I had nothing negative left to tap on or to use the four little questions on that was actually bothering me, so I decided to have a look at my need to save everybody. I pretty quickly made the connection with what I had seen in the Inna Segal book a few days previously – I was not liking something in my environment. I didn't like to see people ill and suffering. Could this be the problem?

I went to the bedroom, lay down on the bed and started to do The Work on the statement, "I need to help people to get well." I applied Byron Katie's four magic questions, and it went something like this:

"Are you sure you need to help people?" Well, yes, kind of. I need to pass on this knowledge, don't I?

"Are you absolutely sure you need to help people?" Hmm... Well, no. Perhaps not.

"How does this thought make you feel?" It makes me feel like I can never really relax in somebody's company, as I always want to tell them about their diet or their life choices. I feel agitated all the time that people are sick and they don't know how to get well. I feel exasperated with the powers that be still perpetuating lies about what's healthy and what isn't.

"How would you feel without this thought?" I'd feel a lot more carefree and at peace. I could go about my day without wanting to interfere in other people's business.

So then I started to turn it around: "I shouldn't tell people how to get well." "They should be ill..." etc., etc.

Suddenly it all became clear! I saw just how much worrying about others took up my time and attention, and above all how much being ill had helped me. It had been the best thing that had ever happened to me. It had taken me to amazing wisdom that I would never otherwise have discovered. It had deepened all my relationships. It had pretty much taken me from being an overgrown child to being a man. In that moment the whole universe changed again. I hadn't realised just how big a stress this had been for me for so long. It really wasn't up to me to save the planet. The planet was doing exactly what it needed to do, as were all the people on the planet. I just wasn't my business; I could let go. Of course I could still talk to people about it especially if they asked, but it would never again be a compulsion and a stress; it would be a privilege and a pure pleasure, and I could let go of the outcome. If somebody was ill, it was probably the perfect thing for them at the time. If they wanted to listen to me harping on about healing themselves, fine, but if not, also fine... In the words of Dr. Jack Kruse, "You can lead a horse to water, but you can't guarantee it won't piss in it."

How could I have missed this for so long? How could I have carried around such an obvious burden? What an idiot!

Then something absolutely astonishing happened. As I watched my old beliefs and stress about this subject fall down, they took more with them – related sub-beliefs and some that even appeared not to be related at all. I saw them all collapsing like countless trees falling in a forest. Soon the forest was all but gone, and all that was left was my heart. I had a flashback to a dream I'd had when very ill in which some clay or whatever it was that was covering my heart had cracked away, revealing it shining and clean – a glimpse of what was possible, or, indeed inevitable?

I couldn't move. I was pinned to the bed and nothing of me was left except for absolute howling bliss blowing through the void, dissolving my body and opening my heart until I was expanded to the size of the universe, and all I was made of was pure love. I didn't move from the bed for a good two hours while this raged through me, cleaning and purging as it went. Eventually the expanded awareness subsided, and I was back in my body on the bed. I slowly got up and sat on the edge of the bed. I knew that nothing would ever be the same again.

It wasn't that I had learned or experienced anything more or different than I had that day when I sat on the wall in my back garden eight years previously. I was transported to the same awareness of unity, but this time I was experiencing it though my heart, and it was a warm and loving experience as opposed to the cold, heartless realisation in the garden.

I sat there for a long time, and the tears came in floods. I was home. This was maybe what Roger Linden had talked about when he mentioned stabilisation all those years previously. Scenes from the previous three years ran through my head, and I saw what a long journey it had been from "here" to "here".

I no longer cared whether people were ill or not. I no longer cared whether they meditated or not. It was either their business or god's business – not mine. I could let go. I fell in love with myself, everyone else and even disease. I fell in love with my own limitations and stupidity. I fell in love with my mother's eccentricities. I fell in love with my painful eye and my remaining niggling joints. I fell in love with myself not falling in love with everything. I fell in love with the whole beautiful, ecstatic, hilarious, shitty, agonising, inspiring, terrifying thing that is life. I fell in love with the universe.

In short, I fell in love with "what is".

It was utterly beautiful.

A few days later, I had to go back to the hospital for an injection right next to the eyeball to carry the steroid solution to where the drops had failed to penetrate so it could work its anti-inflammatory magic on the retina. I didn't know if it would work, and neither did they for sure. When I was lying there having the needle stuck into my eye, I saw puzzlement in the faces of the two doctors and the nurse present that I seemed so happy and peaceful, which I was. I was so grateful to my eye for leading me to this amazing letting go that I found myself totally detached from the outcome. Of course it would be nice if the procedure worked and it saved my sight, but if I lost an eye would it all have been worth it? Oh yes! Where it had led me would have been worth it 100 times over. I had no regrets.

As it turned out I was lucky. I regained my sight perfectly in that eye... weirdly, perhaps to an even better standard than it had been before. Was it the injection that did it, or was it clearing that huge emotional block? I will never know and I really don't care... All I know is that I feel like the luckiest person alive. How could a total idiot like me have been so lucky to be shown the universe in this wonderful light?

Now, I'd like to say at this point that the above tale of further awakening might seem very empty and trivial to some readers, many of whom I am sure have either never had this issue or who cleared it years ago as a simple matter of growing up. But this is my point: such emotional blockage clearances can often be triggered by something that on its own seems rather insignificant, or, like mine, something that I really should have noticed years previously. Hindsight is 20/20 though, and it's so easy for me to see now. I recount this story to perhaps inspire the reader not to give up and to give consideration to things that might seem inconsequential, or that might even be character traits that you have become so accustomed to over the years that you don't see them as a problem.

From that day on I never needed to consciously use EFT or The Work again. If an uncomfortable thought came up it was just zapped straight away. It was like I had a force field around me that didn't allow such thoughts more than a second to affect me. Of course all the same thoughts still came up, and they still do, but now I don't believe them at all. They take form, present themselves, I notice them and see if they need any attention, and if they are just chattering of the monkey mind they are dismissed.

I also started to count my blessings. I mean, not in a forced way as the self-help gurus will tell you that you need to, but spontaneously. My relationship with my family became so much better, and any little problems or conflicts were greatly lessened and not taken seriously at all. I began to notice the miracles in everything, like everything was made of god. I felt devotion to anything and everything because it was just part of the magnificent whole playing out perfectly through this imaginary construct of habits, impressions and nonsense that is Phil.

Gratitude even flooded in spontaneously for my body and my illness. Not long previously, I would look in the mirror at how skinny I had become, and particularly how my left knee looked a bit odd from the inflammation, and I'd be disgusted. I'd try to look at my reflection and say, "I love you" like the self-help theories advise, but I could barely form the words, let alone feel them deeply. Now though there was nothing but love... love for the battle scars on my body and love for the process of ill health for bringing me to such a beautiful realisation. My swollen knee now became a magnificent reminder of how lucky I had been and how beautifully the universe works – not an unsightly reminder of pain.

Gratitude alone is fantastically healing, and there are many accounts of people healing just from expressing true gratitude. It might be possible to force gratitude to appear, as some techniques suggest, but for me it didn't; it unfolded spontaneously after other blocks were cleared. Still, when it did arrive it accelerated healing considerably. I recently heard a wonderful saying that sums up the power of gratitude: "Imagine that you will wake up tomorrow with only the things you showed gratitude for today."

From then on, unsurprisingly, things took a turn for the better anyway, and my body started to fix the damage and fill out again so I didn't look like a walking skeleton. This was also the stage where I found I could start to reintroduce some of the foods I had not been able to tolerate, and suddenly they caused me no pain or discomfort.

Life became an utter delight. I could switch between "levels" if you like, although all apparent levels are part of the same thing. I could watch a group of people, for example, and see them as just bodies interacting, the way they related to the universe itself, and also that they didn't actually exist and all was just the play of consciousness enjoying itself. My world became one of delicious paradoxes, and I saw how all opposing viewpoints and seemingly contradictory happenings are fine and just how it's all supposed to be. Of course I still advise people about diet (as long as they ask or show an interest), and I still take up a position on one side of a discussion, but I don't have any concept of right and wrong as such anymore. I just do and say what my heart tells me is the most enjoyable, and I have respect for other people's views on anything, as they are neither right nor wrong; they just maintain the balance with other views.

We have created this bizarre state where we live by sense of right and wrong and moral codes, when actually the whole, the universe, or god if you like, cares nothing for any of this. It might seem like a dangerous way to think, and the average person says, "Ah, but if we all thought like that it would be chaos and everyone would be killing each other." I understand that concern, but it just isn't like that. It all becomes a matter of love and you don't harm anyone because you feel so much love for them; in fact they are made of love... everything is. They are part of you, so why would you want to hurt them any more than one of your feet would want to stamp on your other foot?

It becomes apparent that everything uncomfortable, from disagreements to illness, are just constructs of our own making... and at this point I can tell you a secret...

The beast does not exist; it never did. That is its nature – it's a fantasy.

It becomes apparent that healing was never about improving the individual, but noticing that the individual does not really exist as we thought it did. If you take away the constructs that we have built up about ourselves, we can see through to what we really are... just a part of the cosmic computer, or "sense organs of the infinite" rather than separate entities... and then, when the body is free from the stresses of the mind thinking it's an actual individual, it tends to sort itself out and conditions vanish.

It's like becoming a clean slate. Everyone has this idea of "waking up" to be some sort of state of omniscience, but it's actually quite the reverse. You feel like a little baby again in a whole new world – one that was there all the time right in front of you, but which you were too busy being you to notice.

There is a game I like to play now, in which I take away any labels from objects as I look at them. It seems to happen spontaneously while I'm driving and is far more entertaining than the radio during a car journey. I pretend that I'm an alien just turned up here, or maybe a newborn baby who has no idea that the moving shapes and colours are roads, trees, cars etc. As you lose the labels, it becomes far easier to see that it is all just one thing seething and churning and making love to itself. It's a magical, wonderful feeling to see oneself as part of this unfathomable mass of beauty where a steering wheel becomes as beautiful as a bird swooping over the road or a colourful sunset in the rear view mirror. You start to see that everything we do or every code we live by is just a construct. We praise babies for when they learn things and become more like us, but we are actually dragging them from grace, if you like.

The real magic comes though when you have been dragged from grace, but then notice grace with all the other nonsense superimposed upon it. Then what a marvellous playground the world becomes. Sometimes I wonder how I don't cause an accident as I drive along these days! But rest assured, all driving skills still seem to be intact, however far I go into the oneness!

So am I "done"? Have I become some sort of perfect being? No, not at all. I would be surprised if such a thing was possible. It's an ongoing process of keeping the clouds to a minimum so you can still see the blue sky beyond, so to speak. These are days when there are a lot of clouds, but once one knows for sure they are set against a backdrop of blue sky, one does not really worry about them. They come and go, as does everything else in life, and one learns to have total trust that it's all okay and everything, to coin a phrase, is unfolding as it should.

Every day it unfolds a little more. My capacity for appreciating beauty and delight increases, and the wonder of it all never ceases to amaze me. But now I know that it's the wonder of the whole lot appreciating itself, and I am just a tiny little aspect of it all. One cannot just jump into this positivity by straining at it or posting affirmations on the fridge – one has to chase, or more accurately, surrender to, the ultimate goal – to realise the nature of who "you" actually are, then everything else falls into place.

In reading this section one might be tempted to think that it's necessary to pursue positivity and happiness, but they are merely the by products of what is so elusive and formless I cannot describe it any better than anyone else who has tried down the ages. All we can do is tell people what it feels like to the individual when what we really want to get across is that there is no individual in the first place. Then we are just left with telling people what it's not.

So, are my emotions in perfect balance now? No, of course not, but they don't affect me very much, and I find my failings funny rather than agonising about them. I find little things to work on every day too, and new ones appear all the time. They are much easier to disperse when they are new than when they are ingrained over years or decades though. But, I have definitely cleared the ones that gave me the worst stresses. I've zapped all the major enemies, and I have seen the miracles of healing that can happen when you do so. Now, though, I have a totally different view of problems and pain. If a thought comes up that disturbs me for some reason there is an almost instant automatic inbuilt "zapper" that takes it down.

It's like Byron Katie's four questions are automatic in me. Well, I seldom need to get beyond a very simple, "Are you sure?" and the nonsense tends to crumble. I certainly never blame anything on anyone anymore, not even on myself; it's just "what's happening". The process of identifying and zapping false beliefs and daft emotions as they appear is actually a fun game now. So, I can honestly say that I even enjoy problems. You will never get rid of problems, so learning to love them is really the only way to realise the dream of being problem-free, and the good news is it's in your hands! Nobody else can help or thwart you.

So where am I now as I write this, physically speaking? What's the bottom line to this story for somebody who might still be ill and needs inspiration? Am I totally cured? Well, all my niggling ailments that I listed in part one and which led up to it getting into my joints have vanished 100%. Most of the affected joints have completely healed up and any damage that could be felt or was visible has reversed itself. If I do eat the "wrong" foods or abuse my body in some other way I still have a slight niggle in my left knee and my right wrist. This is so mild, at worst 5% of what it was when I was very ill, it never really bothers me at all and does not cause pain – it's just a little stiffness and tingling. However, this is fine, as I know what it's about, and it doesn't stop me doing anything I want – long walks, mountain biking, weight training, energetic and lengthy gigs on the drums. My body feels better than it ever has before.

Knees are to do with moving forward in life, and at the time of writing I still have some issues about money. My situation now is that I have a new baby and not much income or stable profession. My life situation with my family and my music is wonderful, but I know I have issues with money and providing for them. I wake at 3am and worry about how we will support ourselves, but as I said, it's nothing like before. I notice the distress happening, and it's gone in a moment – I just let it stay long enough to remind me it needs attention. It's still enough to cause the smallest of problems in related body parts, as my genetics for arthritis are still there, but now I'm grateful to it for being part of my "instrument panel" that helps me to clear issues. I have a sensitive instrument panel!

In fact these last niggles made me postpone the writing of this book, as I felt I had to be 100% perfect before I had any authority to tell anyone else about this, but now I see that's a bit silly. Perfection is something we are never likely to attain, even if such a thing exists. I am still alive, which means that of course I have work to do. I realised that maybe this book will lead to more income and an idea of what I will do "when I grow up", so I had to admit that it was a bit of a Catch-22 situation. Do I wait until I'm totally healed, or do I throw myself into writing this book, because it might well be the last piece of the puzzle in my healing – knowing that I am following my heart in helping people with these conditions, and in doing so, finding my life path and "moving forward" on it.

Actually, it has already started from my website, Facebook, Twitter and my Buddha at the Gas Pump interview reaching a lot of people, which I was so honoured to be asked to do, and which is still available online. Along with getting back into drumming, as previously mentioned, helping people with consultations over the phone or Skype has already made yet another improvement to those last two joints, so I know it's also something to do with supporting myself and finding my dharma. I have never done anything in my life with money as a prime motivator; in fact I have totally ignored it, and I know it's something I need to address, as my silly previous ideas of it being something evil are nonsense. I now see it as all part of the whole anyway.

⮕ Chapter 13
THE BLESSING OF SUFFERING

The first thing that anyone notices about an illness of any sort is suffering. From a runny nose to terminal cancer, when the body misfires it's never very pleasant. Nowadays we are taught that suffering is bad and it needs to be stamped out as much as possible. Doctors prescribe drugs to cover physical symptoms and psychiatrists smash down the psychological ones. With all this covering up of suffering there must be a huge collective lid ready to blow off when the pressure reaches a certain point.

Many of the so-called self-help gurus are even banging on about focusing on the positive and rejecting the negative. This all adds up to creating a society that is so afraid of pain and suffering that if they stub their toe they think it's the end of the world. I sympathise – I remember the early days of my diagnosis and the pure horror it held for me. But now I see suffering in a totally different light.

It took me many years – decades in fact – to begin to value suffering. I noticed that all the best things happened to me after a period of suffering. This is just the way the universe works. Hard work is followed by financial reward, long hours of practice precede virtuosity on an instrument, and the pain of labour is followed by the gift of a child. Sometimes you just have to grit your teeth and pull that splinter out to avoid infection. It might hurt in the short term, but in the long run you will be better off.

We all have our own levels of deafness to the messages that the body and the universe send us. Many people wiser than me get a slight physical niggle and adjust their diet or lifestyle slightly to correct this. Then there are people who are stone deaf (or who just have selective hearing maybe) like me who wait decades, ignoring the messages that the body send until a full-blown disease manifests. We are not taught to listen, so this situation is perpetuated. Doctors tell us not to try and diagnose ourselves and to just take a pill to kill the discomfort. Very often they mock if you mention that you have done your own research. It's a strange way to look at health care – everything is upside down. Now, I'm not saying that life is hard and it's just one battle after another; it does not have to be like this at all. My main aim for writing the third part of this book is to show that there is a place inside that is so much more profound than regular happiness so the periods of suffering seem pretty mild. This place has always been there, but the chaos of our surface existence has covered it up, so we identify with this little body we are borrowing so much that each little setback is some kind of disaster.

Now that I know – not believe, but know – that at the subtlest level there is only one organism (the universe, god or consciousness if you like, whichever term you prefer) and the phenomenal world is just the film projected on the screen of that organism, then periods of happiness and periods of suffering are not really judged as good or bad. Actually, since most "bad" events lead to much "better" conclusions, judging any event as good or bad seems nonsensical.

I was lucky in that I got my life back, but I didn't get my life back until I totally accepted that it would be okay if I never did get it back. When you reside more in the universe that's looking out through the eyes than you do in the brain behind the eyes, death also loses its terror. The old cliché that we are immortal starts to make sense. We are probably not individually immortal, but the ocean that we are a drop of is immortal. I no longer believe in reincarnation or linear time for that matter – too many strange things have happened in the course of my healing journey for me to see things in black and white ever again. However, I have a feeling that when somebody dies, it's like pouring a cup of water back into the bath that you scooped it up from. You can scoop another cup, and it might well contain some of the same water droplets/molecules as the previous cup, but they will be mixed up with new ones. Perhaps this is how we get past life memories – which are probably more accurately parallel lives anyway.

Complete surrender to the universe and trust that it knows best is a very important stage in healing. It is also an important stage in dying, as not everyone heals. There is nothing wrong with dying – sometimes despite people's best efforts, it is time for them to go, and finding a way to be at peace with that is so important. So what can we do to get to such a place? I'm sorry, but here I'm going to have to let you down somewhat, as I don't have the answer to that question. I spent years and years in meditation, but it did not take me there. It's a great help in easing the experience of life, but it didn't wake me up. I have listened to so many awakened people speaking about all sorts of aspects of this subject, and I still cannot figure out what the recipe for awakening is.

I would recommend listening to as many masters as you can. Start with Adyashanti, Rupert Spira, Mooji, Tony Parsons, Paul Hedderman etc and just see where the rabbit hole takes you. You will probably find that some resonate with you and others don't. This is fine, but do listen. The inspiration gleaned from their words can be profound.

I would also highly recommend the interviews that Rick Archer does on his online show "Buddha at the Gas Pump". The fact that so many of these people are "ordinary" makes it so much more accessible to the average person, demystifying what has been seen as something very exclusive for time immemorial. As well as having had the great honour of being asked to do one in May 2015 (number 290), I have listened to all (at the time of writing) over 300 of them. I have been very fascinated to hear the tales of people who have experienced such awakenings, and just how many of them got ill just before, during or after the event. I have been looking for a common thread that runs through their tales to see if there is one thing that actually triggers such a shift of awareness. It doesn't appear to be spiritual practice necessarily, because there are many who have woken up spontaneously with no previous interest in anything spiritual. But then again, did they inherit some accumulated good karma from their own past lives (or some shared droplets from other people's past lives maybe). Who knows?

The three things that have often added up to the perfect storm are: firstly, an intense desire throughout your life to find the answer to life's mysteries; secondly, a moment of true surrender, and thirdly, suffering. This is certainly how it was for me, but again, there are always exceptions to the rule. We definitely need to reframe our attitude towards suffering if we are ill though. We need to see it for the potential gift that it is. Find a place where you can be happy even if the illness stays with you forever. Once you find that place, you will have far more of a chance of recovery anyway. Surrender – don't fight it. Let it reveal its secrets. Fighting anything is useless. If you are hitting somebody they will not become your friend and will probably attack you back. Give them kindness, appreciation and space and they will open up to you. Treat your illness as a dear friend who has come to give you an important message.

If there's one thing that can help you to find a place of peace no matter what is happening externally, I would suggest that it is a matter of subtraction. Just as I wrote about diet and environmental issues in part two of this book, it's usually far more powerful to subtract the things that are causing us distress than it is to add something extra. This is why the process of self-enquiry in its many forms is such an effective tool. If you use it to clear all the thoughts and beliefs that are troubling you, it's very likely that the truth of your essential nature will be revealed naturally in due course. There's not much point looking for the horizon if you are still in a forest. Wait until the trees thin out or you get to higher ground and then you might have a chance. However, if you are in the middle of the trees, learn to love them too.

When out of the forest, we can see clearly that we create our realities, and indeed our illnesses. Well, it's not actually us as individuals, but us as sense organs of the infinite, chips in the cosmic computer. Nothing in creation is permanent apart from change, so rest assured that however bad you might feel at the moment, it will not... cannot... last forever. Resisting will slow progress in anything, so just relax, let the universe take its natural course, and whatever outcome appears, it will surely appear quicker and more smoothly than if you fight it. Just be with the pain and discomfort... quietly let it wash over you and reveal its secrets. It might take you to a revelation about your character, or it might take you to something as simple as a useful website that's relevant to your next step. It's all part of the magic. So what about people who heal spontaneously, or at least seemingly spontaneously? I wasn't so lucky, although some of the stages in my healing happened so suddenly after long plateau phases that they seemed downright miraculous. Many people sit around hoping for a miracle, and this causes them to do nothing. Okay it's possible, and there are many documented accounts (look into Anita Moorjani's late stage cancer recovery story for some great inspiration), but you cannot rely on it.

Some of the more spiritual types who I came into contact with during my healing journey used to say words to the effect of, "It's possible to heal spontaneously, so why mess around with all this diet and stuff?" To answer that, I would say to keep an open mind about what's possible, and you might very well get lucky and have a sudden and total remission, but in the meantime, you might just as well do something practical about it. The worst that can happen is that the methods I detail in the book will give you extensive relief from the symptoms and put you in a mindset where secrets about you will be revealed.

Anyway, very often when you look at these stories of spontaneous remissions, it turns out that they were not so spontaneous after all. Anita Moorjani for example had an awakening and made a critical decision while in a coma that brought her back. Once all the stresses that cause illness are taken away, the body can heal very fast, and this is often seen as spontaneous, but what is often not seen is the process that led up to it. I hope I have given you some ideas to kickstart that process in you.

I wish you all the best of luck and great joy and success in your healing journey.

➲ Chapter 14
MY HEALING JOURNEY IN WORDS AND PICTURES

Here is a simple before and after shot. The pic on the left was taken in about 2009 when I decided I should get myself back into shape. Instead I got even worse, and by 2010 I was crippled with arthritis. The pic on the right was taken sometime in 2011 to deliberately mimic the first one for a great comparison. At that time I had lost about five stone (70lbs) and the majority of my plethora of niggling ailments. The joints were still not perfect, but the improvement is clear to see.

Next, here's a seven-photo journey through my healing from psoriatic arthritis and many other associated ailments connected with autoimmunity and inflammation 1. (Dreadlocks, fat, top left) Early 2010, just before I got really ill. I weighed around 15 stone (210lbs). Ten years of neglect after being in very good shape and quite lean at 14 stone (196lbs) back in 2000 had left me with all sorts of issues from bad digestion to the rumblings of what was to become crippling joint inflammation by October/November that year. I took this photo as a "before" hoping to get back into shape with diet and exercise and chart my progress on my website. Little did I know things would get far worse before they got better, but what a learning curve it was!

2. (Dreadlocks, skinny, top middle) Summer 2011, after panicking from the onset of the arthritis, briefly taking the nasty conventional meds and getting obsessed with juicing, fasting and being raw vegan. By this time I weighed about 10 stone (140lbs). I'd lost all the remains of my muscle, and I was still full of inflammation, brain fog and depression. I was very arthritic and inflamed with no chance of training to rebuild the lost muscle.

3. (Sitting, bottom left) January 2012 on a holiday to Thailand, still about 10 stone (140lbs), but this shows how inflamed the ankles were. Walking was nasty unless dosed with painkillers. I might be smiling for the photo, but life wasn't much fun most of the time.

4. (Getting out of pool, bottom middle). Spain, summer 2012. This is the photo that really shocked me. Oddly, I am better here, having discovered GAPS and reintroduced protein, and I was running on fats rather than sugars, but being in ketosis burned the last of the fat and left me weighing 9 stone (126lbs) and looking like a skeleton. Although there is less pain, the damage can be seen – left knee very swollen, quad muscle all but gone. It was a low point, but when you hit rock bottom you can think about bouncing back.

5. (Red shorts, top right). Autumn 2012, Spain again. The return to health begins. Much improved, and the switch from veganism to high fat/low carb and some protein had me maybe weighing 10 stone again with no increase in body fat. Two days later I was screaming in Granada A&E with a big kidney stone stuck in my ureter, but systemic inflammation was massively reduced.

6. (Drums, middle right). Summer 2014. Gradually inflammation died down, allowing me a winter of weight training (2013/14), which had put some of the muscle back. Introducing a few carbs in the spring, which took me out of ketosis, had brought a little fat back, but I was in pretty good shape, weighing maybe 11.5 stone (161lbs). I was back playing drums, which I never thought I'd be able to do. I was feeling great, and a lot of the emotional issues had been addressed, which are at the root of autoimmunity. By then there was absolutely no trace of the disease in my ankles, with just a little niggle in left knee and right

wrist, but getting better every day.

7. (Bottom right, mirror selfie). Spring 2015. Another winter of weight training had brought back more of my lost muscle. I was feeling even better, but my new mended gut/gut flora allowing me wine and chocolate had put on more fat than I'd have liked and got me to nearly 13 stone over the winter. Still, it was fun! In that photo I weighed about 12.5 stone (175lbs). Joints were good and the damage healing (docs say that's impossible) and even the wasted left quad muscle was growing back nicely. The improvements continue day by day on all levels – physical, emotional and spiritual.

IN CONCLUSION...

Further reading and resources

I have decided not to make a list of links and books etc that you could use to investigate further, as I am always finding out new information and wonderful new people are popping up all the time with their contributions to the healing of the body and the planet. As I find them, I post links to them online, so if you want to delve deeper, please visit the "resources" page of my website at http://pureactivity.net where you can find links to many of the masters that I mention in this book and much more.

Consultations

I hope you enjoyed this book and that the information has given you the knowledge and confidence to take control of your own health.

If you would like any more help, I also do consultations, details of which are also on the website. It would be a pleasure to hear from you.

Wishing you health and happiness.
Phil.

Testimonials

"It was really great meeting and working with Phil – what a life changer!"

"Thank you so much Phil! This is really a major breakthrough for me and my health, and I am so grateful to have heard your story and for the time you've taken to guide me in this."
    (Excerpts from the testimonials and success stories below...)

*

"I've been reading and listening and educating myself and finding my way, the main motivator being how much stronger and less inflamed I feel already! People keep telling me how much better I look and have I lost weight etc. The pain in my joints is

dramatically reduced and I can feel my strength coming back in my yoga practice. For the first time in months I was able to get up into a full wheel this week (my wrists just wouldn't take the weight since the virus hit me). This was really joyous for me! I've done a lot of chiropractic and massage as well as everything else to try to deal with Chikungunya virus and subsequent inflammation etc. I went for a massage last week and a chiropractic attunement today and both my chiropractor and massage therapist commented on how much the inflammation had gone down in my spine and joints! I feel like my body has responded so fast and so well that I must be on the right track! I'm feeling more hopeful that I can find my way (having also watched a bunch of people talking about vegan paleo which I know sounds insane), but for me I am realizing that the main thing was to get the inflammatory foods out of my diet and adding fish, eggs for more protein and fat feels more doable and I feel more trust in myself and life to guide me. I won't ever go back to a diet so heavily based on grains and legumes. Thank you so much, Phil! This is really a major breakthrough for me and my health, and I am so grateful to have heard your story and for the time you've taken to guide me in this. Sorry to be so long winded, but I wanted to share my joy!" – Katie C

*

"I have gradually changed my diet since we spoke... it's a good journey. I have more or less given up grains. LOVING the broths and big chunks of fatty red meat! It certainly feels good to eat more fat... which brings me to what I am finding... It feels like I am starting to be able to tell how my digestive system / body "feels" about what I dump in it, and I get a pretty immediate energy response. This seems to be the way, as it ends the confusion that is inevitable with so many different and often contradictory ways and means to health. One thing I've noticed is how much I am enjoying food. The loss of appetite is changing to healthy enjoyment. I had bacon, tomatoes and avocado the other day – OMG, absolutely scrumptious!" – Nick W.

"It was really great meeting and working with Phil – what a life changer! I was feeling tired all the time, bloated and feeling that my body was slowing down and worn out. I was getting old, and I'm only 51. Phil suggested some changes to my diet and put me on a plan, and after a few weeks it all turned around. I even lost over a stone in weight in ten days without even trying to. My energy increased, my focus and attention increased, and I actually feel normal again, or rather like when you're a kid and you just feel OK and ready to go... (although I have to say, I seem to have more energy than my own kids!). My wife is also now involved and is about to start a special plan to help her with her immune system, which has been systematically depleted by repeated antibiotic prescriptions and poor diet. Phil has recommended the GAPS diet for her, and after researching some links from Phil and preparing, she is looking forward to beginning it over the next few weeks. It's amazing how the knowledge and understanding provided by Phil has transformed the way we look at food and how we shop. Nothing overcomplicated – simpler in fact – and I actually enjoy everything I eat and don't miss anything from my old diet... I feel great! No fuzziness, tiredness, bloating or lethargy. Concentration is increasing. I think one of the main things is that I'm actually enjoying cooking now and tasting things, so everyone in the family gets the benefit. Even the kids are into the understanding and feeling positive more often. On the spiritual side, the awareness is easier to maintain, or rather it's more upfront than behind, probably due to the extra energies moving. I can tune in strongly and remain while active at other things... It's always a difficult explanation, but I know you know what I mean." – Wayne C.

*

"When I look back at the last few years it is interesting to note that along with a series of apparent 'awakenings' I experienced a great deal of physical upheaval and changes. It began to dawn on me that these awakenings were going on on every level, very much including the physical level. There was much sickness, and the body was shouting louder and louder – I needed to listen! Phil was somehow a catalyst for me to listen to my body. What made the difference for me was that this was not yet another "health kick"; it

was not coming from a purely physical self-improvement motive, and nothing was being promoted! I only listened to Phil because there is a resonance... not because I was looking for some 'solution' to a health problem. I just had these words pop into my head: "Step aside you dimwit! God wishes to heal himself!" ME always wants to fix it, and there's the beauty – the body is the absolute master of fixing itself! That's what it does!" – Nick W.

*

"Phil has been most enthusiastic and knowledgeable in supporting me to try a whole new inflammation-reduction diet. I have asthma/eczema/bronchiectasis and a likely candida infestation. Phil has really helped me fast track to a diet that will starve any nasty pathogens out of my body. I am still in the early stages of experimenting with this, but so far breathing has improved, and as a bonus I also feel more streamlined and brighter in my spirits. Phil's website also highlighted the Blublocker glasses, which I really like for the computer work I do. Phil has introduced me to some well-informed alternative health networks that I knew were out there but was floundering to find on my own. I recommend if you are struggling with the mainstream NHS system and suspicious that Big Pharma drugs are not quite the ticket that you talk with Phil" – Sarah W.

*

"I have been a strict vegetarian for close to 18 years. For the past 15 years I had quite sensitive (itchy) skin and was diagnosed with an autoimmune condition, which means – one treatment option – some cream (which I never bother to use) and no cure. For the past year my body has been craving for fish and meat, and on a few occasions I could not resist the temptation. (And yes, I felt guilty about falling off the vegetarian wagon!). Also, for the past year the irritation of the skin increased quite a bit, and in addition to that, my joints start hurting to the degree that I felt like a 90-year-old lady instead of being 50 – no energy, no mobility, no fun! Accidentally I heard Phil telling his "arthritis story" on Buddha at the Gas Pump. His story somehow resonated with me. I *immediately wrote to him and had a Skype consultation. Well, it's working for sure! The "magic pot" makes fresh food every day. Eating meat (chicken and organs/beef/pork at this stage/fish/eggs and some veggies mostly). Skin irritation is gone. Joints are happy too. Energy is high, and I even forgot about the need of napping. Also, the food tastes really goooood and feels very fulfilling! Sometimes I still slip into my homemade ice cream, but the body's reaction to sugar is quite unpleasantly fast and strong. I have no doubt that naturally the craving is finding its way out. Really happy, happy about everything!!"* – V. Z.

*

"I first saw Phil Escott on the net being interviewed by Rick Archer. I was impressed with his forthright attitude. He spoke about his health and about "enlightenment." I listened attentively and understood his spiritual path to be an ongoing process of the recognition of the power that inhabits our hearts and minds, and yes, our bodies. Phil has strengthened not only this recognition, but as a consequence, has also successfully strengthened his body. The low carb, high fat version of the paleo diet has been a prime source for his recovery from a lifetime of inappropriate eating habits, which we are all subject to. He surmounted this difficulty, and has generously shared with me all the valuable information that was needed to bring him to success. Presently he is my main source. I am deeply indebted to him for his presence in my life at this time."
– Joan F.

*

"Basically the main diet changes have been: no spuds or bread (made with grains). This is the biggest change, as I was previously eating quite a lot of these. Big increase in red meat and fat, increase in veg, some sauerkraut almost every day. Smoking, tea and coffee addiction continues, but using only organic cream and raw honey instead of raw sugar and milk. No heartburn and no chemical tablets taken since a few days before we Skyped, and I feel much better – more energy, no nausea, which was happening quite a bit, and no sign of those weird passing out turns. So it seems it was most auspicious I chanced upon you at a perfect time

and some things just fell into place with very little effort. Oh yes, as I said, I have been enjoying food and eating, even organising making the food (which has been a big problem) has become much more doable and enjoyable. So thank you so much, dear Phil... Lots of love here!!" – Nick W.

Printed in Great Britain
by Amazon